OLD TIMES

IN

WEST TENNESSEE.

REMINISCENCES—SEMI-HISTORIC—OF PIONEER LIFE
AND THE EARLY EMIGRANT SETTLERS IN
THE BIG HATCHIE COUNTRY.

BY
A DESCENDENT OF ONE OF THE FIRST SETTLERS.

MEMPHIS, TENN.:
W. G. CHEENEY, PRINTER AND PUBLISHER.
1873.

RESPECTFULLY DEDICATED

TO THE

SURVIVING PIONEER SETTLERS,

WHOSE BRAVE HEARTS AND STRONG ARMS

Subdued the Wilderness of West Tennessee, and made it the fitting abode for refined, civilized enjoyment,

AND THEIR

IMMEDIATE SUCCESSORS.

PREFACE.

THIS book is prefaced by its title page, requiring but little to be said as to the design of the writer, or his motives for writing it.

It is hardly necessary for the author to put in a *disclaimer* that he assumes to be neither a historiographer nor a biographer, much less an annalist; semi-historic, irregular and defective, if you will, is the only title he claims for it.

Whether it be accorded or not, it is none the less true that "every man has his own style, as he has his 'own nose;' and it is neither polite nor Christian to rally a man about his nose, however singular it may be"—a fact pregnant with homely sense, and commends itself to the exercise of charity on the part of the critical reader.

Conceived when gout most troubled, and born of necessity, it was written when afflicted with physical pain, amply recompensed, however, in the pleasurable interest it gave in reviving the scenes and recollections of his boyhood days. Should the reader derive a tithe of the interest in reading that was afforded in writing, the author will be doubly recompensed.

An apology is due the theme it purports to treat, and is beseechingly asked for the author, for having written it hurriedly and without sufficient data. He had written to many of the immediate successors of the first and early settlers in the Big Hatchie country for something of the early lives and connecting incidents of their brave fathers and people, in subduing the wilds of West Tennessee; but, for some cause or other, except in a few instances, he received no response; possibly they feared to trust such a priceless heritage to the pen of unknown authorship.

It is to be regretted, as their names and heroism in hewing down the forest and opening up the way to thrift and refined civilized enjoyment would have contributed greatly to the interest of the history of OLD TIMES IN WEST TENNESSEE.

The author, not wishing to "play showman to his own machinery," submits the following pages to the reader for what they are worth, with a prayer that he be gentle and deal lightly, and, if merit there be, encourage him to a wider field, yet lying fallow in its virgin freshness.

THE AUTHOR.

CONTENTS.

CHAPTER V.

CHAPTER VI.

CHAPTER VII.

CHAPTER VIII.

CHAPTER IX.

CHAPTER X.

CHAPTER XI.

CHAPTER XII.

CHAPTER XIII.

CHAPTER XIV.

OLD TIMES

IN

WEST TENNESSEE.

CHAPTER I.

Reminiscences—Semi-Historic—of Pioneer Life and the Early Emigrant Settlers of the Big Hatchie Country.

THE poetic vision of the Greek, in looking back through dim antiquity, when Ilion resisted the thunder-bolts of Agamemnon's hosts; when the Argos, freighted with human life, weighed anchor and sailed away to the far-off Colchis; the more modern romances of Fernando DeSoto, Juan Ponce de Leon, Pocahontas and her Captain Smith, Daniel Boone and Tecumseh, is not more thrilling in interest to the descendents of the pioneer settlers of this country than the land of the Chickasaws and Davy Crockett—the Obion, Forked Deer and the Big Hatchie country—when in the cradle of the wilderness.

On the banks of a beautiful creek, north of the Big Hatchie River, in the early days of March, little less than three score years ago, my father pitched his tent, and called it home. There the abode of civilization was first planted in that trackless wilderness. Then but a lad of less than twelve summers, the haunts of the countless wild beasts which filled the land are as freshly mapped out as if it were but yesterday. The frightful howl of the wolf, and the sharp, startling scream of the panther, became as familiar as household words.

'Twas there in childhood I played;
In the untrodden wilderness I strayed;
Land of my youth, whose memories last,
Linking the present with the past.

Thither my father moved from the sands of the old settled part of Mississippi, south of latitude 32°, a distance of more than three hundred miles, through a wild, trackless, savage territory. The fatigue and peril of moving a large family of white and black, through a savage wilderness, with all the paraphernalia of comfortable living, in those days of rude travel, was an undertaking requiring almost superhuman endurance and inflexible will, but my father proved himself equal to it.

In January, 18—, through the lonely vistas of the pine woods, was seen a long train of movers. In front rode my father, on his faithful and sure-footed dapple-gray mare, with heavy holsters swinging across the pommel of his saddle, with their black bearskin covering. Stern, thoughtful and reticent, with indomitable will, he had resolved to convoy his precious charge safely through whatever of peril or difficulty that should menace him. Following close behind was a large black carryall, containing mother, grandmother and the young children. The carryall (ambulance it would be called now-a-days) my father had made in North Carolina, with an eye single to its usefulness as a sleeping apartment, as well as traveling vehicle; long and broad, deep sides and high back, with heavy leather curtains, lined with thick, green baize, when closely buttoned down, and bed made up in it, was comfortable enough for an emperor's wife. It was the traveling and sleeping apartment of my mother, grandmother and three young sisters.

Provident in arrangement, my father had gone to Mobile and purchased a year's supply of everything requisite to a comfortable living in the wilds of the Big Hatchie—coffee, tea, rice, sugar, flour, spices and medicines, cards, cotton and spinning-wheels, every variety and kind of seeds, implements of husbandry, carpenter and blacksmith tools, and assorted nails, not forgetting an ample stock of powder, lead and shot, selecting twenty head of choice milch cows with their calves and yearlings, and about the same number of stock hogs. My mother contributed her share in the necessary preparation for the journey; every one, both black and white, were properly and comfortably clad in homespun clothes—stout overcoats for the men and long jackets for the women. The seats and knees of her boys' pants she padded with dressed buckskin (this economic measure is appreciated by all who have made long journeys, camping out every night). The train, when in motion, presented an imposing appearance. The weather being favorable, the country open pinewoods, now and then a few miles of neighborhood road, which happened to lay in our course, we reached the Choctaw territory at nightfall on the fifth day. There we remained over until Monday. My father considered it necessary to communicate with the chief, and obtain safe conduct through his territory. These little diplomatic arrangements completed, and the services of a guide, or pilot, secured, word was given to *gear up!* The second week opened upon us heading slowly through the Choctaw nation, rumbling over roots and such undergrowth as did not impede travel. We made some days as much as ten miles, oftener, however, not more than six or eight. We were not unfrequently delayed for several days when difficult crossings of streams were to be made. Often it was found impracticable to construct bridges, when floats (pontoons) were made, and the wagons unloaded and taken apart, and everything packed across by hand. All these difficulties were met and overcome with a hearty good will, and songs of good cheer. Marvelous had been the stories told the negroes of the good things in store for them in the Big Hatchie country. That it was literally a land flowing with milk and honey; so rich in soil that you only had to make a hole in the ground with your heel, drop the corn into it, and it would grow without work; the forest hanging with the most delicious fruits, and the ground covered with strawberries; even to fat pigs, ready roasted, and running about with knife and fork in their backs, much of which they wrought into song.

We found the Choctaws friendly and well disposed. My father did not, however, relax his vigil in having a close watch kept upon the stock during the night. The cows and hogs were belled, so as to give the alarm when in the slightest disturbed. The camp was infested with Indians every night, bringing in every variety of game, with other eatables, asking to trade. My father had supplied himself with a good stock of beads and red things. A lively trade was carried on most every night. Venison and wild turkeys were in abundance, with beautiful bead baskets, and every variety of bead-work. A few loads of powder or a red cotton handkerchief would pay for a fat gobbler or a saddle of venison. We fared sumptuously.

Reaching the Chickasaw territory, the Choctaw guide was relieved, my father making him many presents for his faithful services, sending presents to his chief. A Chickasaw guide was engaged, and the course of travel decided upon. To avoid the broken country along the head-waters of the numerous streams flowing westwardly, a more easterly direction was advised.

Leaving the lazy and proverbially filthy Choctaw, we entered the Chickasaw nation—noble race of the red man, first to resist the iron heel of the white man, famed for their bravery and ferocious bearing in war, and among the first to make a generous and lasting peace, and cultivate the arts of civilization. The country through which we traveled was slightly rolling, wood principally oak and hickory, devoid of tangled undergrowth. Traveling for days without incident or difficulty worthy of mention, we reached the thickly settled portion of the nation, in the vicinity of which was situated the principal village, at which the chief resided. It was on a Friday; man and beast needed rest, and the order was given that we would lay over till Monday. No travel was done on the Sabbath. My father, a strict old-side Presbyterian, was true to his faith in "observing the Sabbath, to keep it holy," and required of his family, both black and white, that they should do the same.

The tents were pitched upon a lovely spot, on the margin of a gentle slope overlooking the beautiful prairie to the east, a clear running brook close by. When the bright morning sun rose, chasing the gray mist over the broad expanse of the lovely prairie to the east and northeast, numerous Indian settlements, or villages, were seen in the distance. The village at which the chief resided lay to the northwest of us some six miles. Orders were given to prepare for washing—to Jack and Jim to get out the big kettle and swing it, the washtubs, and stretch the clothes-line, the cattle and hogs to be driven over in the prairie, and a close watch kept upon them.

During the day the chief, accompanied by several of his braves and his interpreter, visited the camp. The interpreter was a negro slave, and belonged to the chief, who owned many slaves. The object of his visit was to invite my father to visit him, extending the hospitalities of the village to the whole camp. A reciprocal trade was carried on during the day. The squaws brought large baskets of corn and pumpkins, some with rice and hominy, others with hickory-nut kernels, carefully picked out, many of them without being broken. The trade was interrupted by the boys coming into camp, delighted with their findings while roaming over the prairie. Everybody's curiosity was excited to see; from a dozen voices at once, "Let me see!" "Let *me* see!" "O, *do let me see!*" The objects of so much curious interest were several white flint arrow-heads and a large corroded leaden ball. Such was the marvel at what had been picked up on the prairie that the chief and his braves, who had been standing seemingly unconcerned, were applied to for something of their history. They certainly had a history; relics of art, of the white and the red man, found side by side in the wilds of a savage country, excite the curious to know something of them. The chief, a huge mass of fat, with a jolly, good-natured face, and an intelligent, laughing eye, shook his big sides with a grunt, and spoke through his interpreter thus: "Long, long ago," pointing in the direction from which the boys came running, "on yonder hill a big battle was fought between the red man and the white man. The red men killed all the white men, since which time the red man has been at peace with the white man." This was the only information obtained to the numerous inquiries as to when, and who were the white men engaged in such deadly conflict with the red men. The rock from which the arrow-head was cut did not exist in this region. The size of the leaden ball differed from the ordinary rifle bullet then in use, and its corroded state excited interest as to its antiquity. My father, thinking he could throw some light upon the subject, spoke, addressing himself to the chief, who had settled himself upon the ground, with his fat legs crossed under him: "That more than two hundred and eighty years ago, Spain, a powerful nation across the big water, sent a great many big ships, with men, arms and ammunition, and fine horses, to take possession of all this country; that they landed somewhere on the coast of Florida, under the command of a great man called Fernando DeSoto; that DeSoto, landing his men, guns and horses, marched up through the territory of the Alabamas, then, turning west, crossed the Tombigbee somewhere near the Chickasaw village, passing through their territory, crossing the Mississippi at the Chickasaw bluffs; that the Chickasaws were offended with the strangers for entering their territory without asking their big chief to smoke the *calumet*, gave them battle, killing a great number; that more than one hundred and ninety years after the Spaniards passed through the territory of the Chickasaws, the French, who claimed all the country on both sides of the Mississippi, from its mouth to the great lakes in the north, became offended with the Chickasaws for taking sides with and helping the Natchez, with whom they were at war, sent Bienville, who was Governor of Louisiana, with a great army of white men and a large number of Choctaws, up the Tombigbee river to drive them from their territory. Bienville, with his soldiers and Choctaw friends, landed near the Chickasaw villages, marched out and had a big fight at Ackia village." (As the name of the village was mentioned, the chief, who, it will be remembered, had taken his seat upon the ground, quick as an arrow from its bow, jumped up with features animated and both arms extended, gesticulating in the direction of a hillock to the northeast of our camp, sparsely wooded, and repeated the name of the village, "Ackia! Ackia!") Resuming, he told the chief that his people defeated the French, killed a great many, and pursued the remainder to their boats; that his people never had been conquered; they were famed in history for their bravery and heroic bearing in war. Delighted with such a glorious account of his nation, he, with his companions, took their leave, making my father promise to come out and eat with him at his village, which he promised to do Monday.

Our tents had been pitched within a few rods of the historic ground upon which the village of Ackia stood, where, more than two hundred and eighty years ago, its red defenders put to flight DeSoto and his bronzed companions, with their golden spurs, where Bienville fought his great battle with the brave Chickasaws, where the ashes of the handsome Chevalier D'Artaguettie and the noble De Vincennes rest in peace, mingled with mother earth. Shall we search for the history of the leaden ball and the white flint arrow-head among those fallen braves, whose names and deeds have made glorious the history of this memorable spot? Let us while away the Sabbath in so pleasing a search.

The Chickasaws gave the French more concern than all the nations of red men combined. They were the implacable enemies of France. Maintaining their independence, they greatly weakened and divided the New Empire. Communication with the lakes in the north, and New Orleans, was in constant danger of interruption by the intrepid Chickasaws. With their cedar barks they were ready to shoot out into the Mississippi. They permitted no settlement upon the eastern shore of the great river. From the Natchez to the Ohio they claimed dominion, and held it against the French, who had mapped out as belonging to France all the country west of the Alleghanies to the Rocky Mountains—that not a rill or brook that flowed from the mountains into the Father of Waters but ran through French territory. Independent and resolute, they had given aid and comfort to the Natchez, whose utter annihilation the French aimed at. In order, therefore, to secure and reduce the eastern valley of the Mississippi, it was necessary to rid themselves of the Chickasaws. To this end Bienville, then Governor of Louisiana, was instructed by the French Government to fit out an expedition equal to the undertaking, and drive them from the territory. After two years' preparation, fresh troops having been sent out from France, Bienville announced himself ready to move with his expedition upon the Chickasaws. He had written to the brave young Chevalier D'Artaguettie, commanding the Illinois department, to gather all the troops, both white and red, under his command, and join him in the Chickasaw territory—to meet him at the Chickasaw village on the last day of March. Prompt to duty, D'Artaguettie, communicating with Vincennes, commanding the Iroquois and tribes on the Wabash, and Montcheval, commanding the Miamis and Dacotahs, he was soon ready and descending the Mississippi with one hundred and thirty white troops and three hundred and sixty red allies. On the 4th of March Bienville left New Orleans with his imposing army, finely appointed and equipped, carrying many cannon. Untoward winds greatly retarded his movements, and he did not reach Mobile until the twenty-third day. Being delayed there on account of the condition of his boats, it was the 1st of April before the expedition commenced its move up the river. Two hundred miles from Mobile, on the Tombigbee, a depot of ammunition and supplies had been estabtablished, where Bienville was to be joined by twelve hundred warriors of the Choctaw tribe. Reaching their depot of ammunition and supplies, after innumerable delays, they found the Choctaws not yet arrived. While there, Bienville reviewing his grand army, his red allies came up to the number of six hundred, adding greatly to the grand military parade. On the 18th of April Bienville resumed his march up the Tombigbee, arriving opposite the Chickasaw village the 23d day of May, a month and twenty-three days behind his appointed time for D'Artaguettie to join him. His first order, however, was to send out scouts to learn something, if they could, of the expedition from the Illinois, and to reconnoiter the villages. Securing his boats, and constructing a rude fortification in front of them, he put his army in motion, with ten days' rations, leaving the commanders of the boats and a squad of soldiers in charge of the cannon, temporarily mounted, camping at the edge of the prairie, some six miles from the village. At early dawn, before the bright rays of the sun rose over the broad expanse of the prairie, dissipating the gray mist rising from the heavy dew upon the wide-spread waves of the tall grass, Bienville put his army in motion. Chivalry, upon their richly-caparisoned steeds, rode with glittering pomp by the side of the quick, earnest step of the broad-shouldered grenadier, and the heavy tread of the Swiss guards. The gayly-dressed volunteers, among whom were many of the "best young bloods" of France, led by the gallant De Lassier, bearing flying banners, with cheering mottoes, worked in gay colors by their lady-loves, inspired by lively martial music, presented an imposing sight. With soul-stirring aspirations, they did not doubt but that it would strike terror into the hearts of the red men upon whom they were marching. Beware, invaders, beware! the red man's ideas of liberty are too deeply rooted in the soil of their "beloved prairies," under which the bones of their fathers lie, to yield without a bloody resistance. Keenly alive to the fate of the Natchez, whose villages had been laid waste by the French, and their great chief, with four hundred of his brave warriors, *manacled*, and transported in chains to the slave markets of the islands (already were several hundred of the Natchez tribe, who had been driven from their homes and heritage, finding shelter in the wigwams of the Chickasaws), the two years in which Bienville had been gathering troops and fitting out his imposing expedition had not been kept a secret from the red men, whose fathers had lived in quiet dominion over their "beloved prairies" for ages before the face of the white man was seen on the continent. They were ready and prepared for the invader.

Before noon Bienville had reached a position in full view of the villages. The troops were ordered to take refreshments. In the meantime, the scouts sent out to learn something of the whereabouts of D'Artaguettie, came in, reporting that nothing whatever could be heard of him or his command, nor could any signs be found of his having been in the country. They reported great commotion going on in the villages during the night, but since daylight not an Indian had been seen; that the villages seemed deserted. All hopes of co-operation from his northern allies being given up, Bienville decided upon an immediate attack. By the aid of his field glass, he was enabled to locate the stronghold of the defenders of the villages. He decided to move upon it at once, appointing Chevalier de Noyan to lead the attacking column, composed of fifteen grenadiers, chosen from each company, forty-five from the volunteers, and sixty from the Swiss troops, retaining two companies of veterans, who had seen service in old France under the gallant Beauchamp. The rest of the command was to follow close in support of the attacking forces. The stronghold of the Chickasaws seemed to be in a row of strongly built mud cabins on the apex of the hillock upon which the village was situated, flanked right and left, front and rear, by mud cabins, separated from each other equi-distant some forty paces. The attacking column moved up steadily under cover of mantelets, borne by a company of negro slaves, until they had reached within a few paces of the first row of cabins, when a well-aimed volley was fired, seemingly from the ground, not exceeding twenty paces in front of them, killing several negroes. Such was the first shock of the bullets, many penetrating through their pent-house fortification, that the negroes became panic-stricken, and, throwing down their mantelets, took to their heels. The undaunted Noyan, giving orders for the combined forces to press closely up in support of the attacking column, reached the first row of cabins, setting fire to the thatched roofs. Pressing past them, he soon discovered that they were vacated, the Indians occupying them, discharging the first volley, had escaped under cover to the next or middle row, from whence there came a perfect hail-storm of bullets, putting his brave soldiers to the earth faster than their places could be filled by fresh troops, himself severely wounded. Such was the rain of leaden death that his brave troops were forced to take shelter behind the first row of cabins. The principal officers of his staff were killed. The Chevalier De Coutre, the pride of the army, lay riddled with bullets, weltering in his blood. De Mortbrum, leading the brave Swiss, fell by his side. De Juzan, in executing the order of the intrepid Noyan—trying to bring to the front the skulking soldiers from behind the cabins—fell pierced with a half-dozen balls. The Choctaws were ordered up, and made a desperate charge to reach the middle row of cabins, but were repulsed with great slaughter. Bienville, from his standpoint, witnessing the work of destruction going on, and fearing the fate of his whole army, sent Beauchamp, with his two companies, with orders to Noyan to bring off what remained of his forces, and as many of his wounded as possible. Rapidly advancing, he did not reach the place where Noyan, though suffering from a painful wound, was rallying his troops for another charge, without losing one officer and several of his men. The Chevalier De Noyan had resolved to share the fate of his brave officers who had borne the brunt of the attack, or reach the second row of cabins. Receiving orders from Bienville to withdraw his forces, disabled and suffering, he turned the command over to Beauchamp, who, quick to comprehend the situation, ordered a hasty retreat. The noble Grondel had fallen pierced with five bullets, and was about to be left for the tomahawk, when one of his brave grenadiers broke from the line and bore him away upon his broad shoulders, receiving the sixth while being carried off the field. Thus was fought what Bienville called the battle of Ackia Village; such the leaden messengers, left by the brave young D'Artaguettie, in the hands of the Chickasaws, to inform him that he had been there—that faithful to his trust, obedient to his orders, he, with his little army, had waited upon the *ground of his appointment;* that powder and ball was all that he left him as a *souvenance* of his sad fate, in which we trace the history of the "leaden ball" which had been corroding on the soil of the prairie for an hundred years.

The Chickasaws had given evidence of their skill in fortifying themselves against their strong enemy. The walls of their cabins were built of wood and mud, covered over with the same material, and well *thatched* with straw and palmetto, so as to shed the rain and keep them dry. The cabins were so constructed, from one another, as to cross their fires when the enemy should press in among them. In the inside of these fire-and-bullet-proof cabins they dug out to the depth of their arm-pits, and made loop-holes on a level with the ground, from which they could fire in perfect safety. Beauchamp, in writing an account of their inglorious defeat, says: "To make an end of the Chickasaw war, it is necessary to have a detachment of workmen—of miners and bombardiers—with implements and instruments necessary to ferret out these savages, who burrow, like badgers, in their cabins, which are very much like ours. Bienville made a precipitate retreat to his boats, consigning his cannon to the waters of the Tombigbee, together with two thousand heavy manacles, which were in reserve to bind the liberty-loving Chickasaws, and transport them from their native prairies to the slave markets. Dispirited, with feverish disappointment, he turned his boats down stream with what remained of his shattered army, never to invade the territory of the independent Chickasaws again."

What of the Chevalier D'Artaguettie, and the red allies of the Northern lakes, whose sad fate was unknown to the retreating and discomfited Bienville? The reader will recollect that we left him descending the Mississippi with his expedition to join Bienville at the Chickasaw village, on the last day of March. We next find him at a point on the Mississippi called *Ecores a Trudomme*, a place not marked on our modern maps. It was most likely at the Chickasaw Bluffs, where Memphis now, in the pride of her city life and commercial prosperity, stands, as below the bluff the country on the Eastern banks of the river must have been overflowed at that period of the year to the "Walnut Hills," upon which Vicksburg now stands. Here we find him on the fourth of March, waiting for Vincennes and Montcheval, who were following him close behind, and Grampree, commanding the Arkansas on the White river. After several days' waiting, he was joined by Vincennes with forty Iroquois warriors, and three hundred and twenty of the Illinois, Miamis and Dacotahs. In his anxiety not to disappoint Bienville, he put his expedition in motion, which then consisted of one hundred and thirty whites, three hundred and sixty red allies under Vincennes, and thirty Arkansians from Grampree's command. By slow marches he had hoped that Montcheval and Grampree would come up with him. We next find him in the heart of the Chickasaw Territory, waiting for his scouts to bring him tidings of Bienville. The time for them to co-operate against the village was rapidly growing near, and yet Grampree and Montcheval had not come up. His red allies were becoming restive, and provisions were getting short. Father Senac, a Jesuit priest, was his comforter, yet the ardent young chevalier was filled with misgivings. While waiting, and before the return of his Indian scouts, a courier arrived in camp, bringing him a letter from Bienville, saying that, owing to innumerable delays and difficulties, it would be the end of April before he could reach the Chickasaw villages. Slowly reading the letter, he rose, handing it, open, to Father Senac, and walked to the end of his tent, repeating: "Not till the end of April! Impossible! In the heart of a ferocious, wily enemy's territory, on a hostile expedition, with less than a fortnight's provisions, impossible! impossible!" Continuing his walk, he came to the headquarters of Vincennes, with whom he took counsel. Father Senac, who regarded D'Artaguettie as the "apple of his eye," followed with Bienville's letter, joining the two brave commanders. He was welcomed as a counsellor. The three were long engaged in discussing the grave question, what to do. Just then the scouts came up, reporting that they had gone beyond the great prairies, to the water of the Tombigbee, and no tidings of the expedition from below were to be found anywhere; that they had reconnoitered the villages, passing around them so cautiously that they did not think "the eye of a Chickasaw had seen them." The question was debated, whether to return to the boats on the Mississippi, then sixty leagues off, or attempt the capture of some of the smaller villages, and secure supplies to last them until the end of April, when relief would be obtained by the arrival of Bienville. The scouts and their red friends advocated the latter course, reporting that they had discovered a village more isolated, containing not more than thirty cabins; that, from its being so quiet, it must be the village in which the Natchez refugees were dwelling; that they thought it easily surprised and taken, when plenty of provisions would fall into their hands; they could then fortify themselves and remain until the arrival of Bienville. To Artaguettie and Vincennes, the argument seemed feasible, and they adopted that course of action. Orders were given to that end, and the early morning dawned upon that brave little army in motion, in the direction of the village, offering so much hope, then a day and a half march to the east. As the last rays of the sun, on the following evening, were lengthening the shadows of the tall hickories, on the high ridges bordering the prairies, Artaguettie, with his companions in arms, came in sight of the village, some two miles distant in the prairie. Beautifully situated on a hillock, the coveted village stood; the soft mellow rays of the god of day were fast receding from the tall wood, lengthening its golden rays across the broad prairies to the east, reflecting golden hues from the straw-covered cabins of the quiet-looking village. Conscious of being unobserved, the command fell back to a small running branch, and rested upon their arms. At midnight Artaguettie, Vincennes and the pious Father Senac met to devise the order of attack. It was arranged that, an hour before day, Vincennes, with his red allies, take a position within

2

carbine range of the village to the east, and lay down in the tall grass and wait for the signal of attack; Artaguettie commanding his white troops to take a position to the west of the village. The hour for movement found the cautious Vincennes, with his three hundred and sixty red men, moving round to the position assigned them, so noiseless and soft the tread of the red warriors that not a blade of grass was ruffled or displaced. Arriving at the appointed place, orders, by signs, were given to lay down, the tall grass waving over them. Artaguettie had moved up to his position behind a large thicket of reeds, out of which gushed a bold spring, forming a murmuring brook, winding its course to the southeast of the village. The last hour of the night was hushed into silence—painful silence; not a stir came up from the village; nought was heard but the pulsations of the hundreds of anxious hearts lying in wait for the signal to attack. All was still —still as midnight sleep. Why this death-like stillness? Had the quick eye of the ever-watchful Chickasaw been drowsy? Was he asleep? Had the tiger left his lair and taken himself to better quarters? Daylight alone would dispel the painful stillness. At the dawn of day the signal to attack was given. Simultaneously rose from the tall grass, not an hundred yards behind where De Vincennes had taken his position, three hundred and fifty Chickasaws. With the war-whoop and yells unearthly, they rushed with ferocious impetuosity upon the red allies, producing such wild confusion among the Miamis and Dacotahs that they took to flight, leaving the forty Iroquois and thirty Arkansas to receive the shock of battle. Bravely they withstood it, fighting hand to hand; out-numbered five to one, they fought with Spartan courage until there was not one of the seventy left to tell the tale of their heroism, worthy a better fate. Vincennes was taken alive. The triumphant Chickasaws, wide awake as to what was going on in the village, pressed in through the approaches from whence the French expected their allies, with such surprising slaughter, that before the sun was fairly above the eastern horizon, the gallant Artaguettie, with fifteen of his command, were all that remained alive. Father Senac might have made his escape, but he braved death to remain with his young friend Artaguettie, who was severely wounded. The flying Miamis and their red friends were pursued with such terrific slaughter that but few reached the Mississippi with their lives. The Chickasaws treated their distinguished prisoners with kind attention, dressing their wounds, and ameliorating their sufferings. Their fate, however, was to them full of painfull misgivings.

More than two thousand pounds of powder, twelve thousand bullets and many guns fell into the hands of the Chickasaws, which, two months later, was skillfully and effectually used against Bienville and his grand army. But what of the white flint arrow-head? May it not have been hurled from the strong bow of the undaunted Iroquois, cut from their native chalk cliffs on the Great Lakes in the north? Who will say that the white flint arrow-head shall not share with the red men of the north the glories of the first battle of Ackia Village?

We return to Artaguettie and his brave companions. A grand council was called, its decision taken, and preparations rapidly going on for its execution. On a hillock near the village "busy life" was seen during the day, after the meeting of the grand council. Stalwart men were seen carrying huge loads of finely split wood, others were driving stakes in the ground, around which several hundred Indians—men, women and children—had collected. It had been decreed, according to a long-established custom of the Chickasaws, to make a *triumphant sacrifice* of their captives by burning them at the stake. When the evening began to grow nigh, the sun, through the purplish, sombre clouds, flitting across the western horizon, reflecting its blood-red rays upon the clear sky in the east, all eyes were anxiously turned toward the village, from whence a grand procession was moving. In front, the handsome young Chevalier D'Artaguettie, who had braved death in every form; by his side, the pious Father Senac; following close behind, the noble De Vincennes and fifteen other victims, escorted by several hundred painted warriors. On the procession moved, ascending the hillock—the same, most likely, where Bienville stood two months later, when he sent his faithful Beauchamp to bring off his shattered army. The moment was hushed into painful silence; the victims were marched to the circle of stakes, one by one. There were seventeen stakes, and yet there were eighteen victims. One by one were tightly bound until the seventeenth stake had its victim. Alone stood by the great chief a brave young soldier of not more than sixteen years. He was reserved to be returned to his white-faced chief, to inform him and his people of the fate of his comrades. In the center of the circle of stakes finely-split wood was piled up as high as the heads of the victims; circling the stakes was a high pile of faggots. Everything being ready, the faggot-master ordered the fire, when an hundred torches were applied, and the *triumphant dance* began, war-songs and yells most hideous. The last rays of the setting sun made lurid the ascending smoke from the savage funereal pyre, and the crackling flames, rising high above the surrounding wood, took the place of the god of day, and the wild chant and frantic dance went on. Thus perished the first attempt of the white man to plant the "iron heel" of despotism upon the native soil of the Chickasaws.

Leaving our beautiful camping-ground on the margin of the prairie, my father directed his course toward the village to redeem his promise—to eat with the chief. The country was an open hickory barren, and but few obstructions were found to impede travel. We arrived at the village by noon. The chief, with his escort, met my father at the edge of the village, conducting him and the entire train in front of his place of dwelling, which was on a broad street running through the center of the village east and west, studded on each side with antiquated looking china-trees, giving quite the appearance of civilized life. A big dinner had been prepared, and everybody, black as well as white, participated in the great chief's regal hospitality.

The chief and his braves talked much of the Big Hatchie country, calling it their hunting-ground, exhibiting many bear and panther skins procured in that region. The chief showed my father great kindness, sending several of his best hunters along with us to kill game and pilot the best route to Bolivar, then an Indian trading-post. Leaving the village an hour before nightfall, we camped at a fine spring. Resuming travel the next morning, it was continued without interruption, our Indian guides bringing in a venison or fat gobbler every day, arriving at Bolivar the last week in February, having been in the wilderness forty days and nights.

Bolivar was then a small trading-post, poorly supplied with goods, wares and merchandise, except such as were profitable in trading with the Indians. My father crossed the river Big Hatchie, and turned down it, following a blaze, digging down hills and making pole ridges until he reached the vicinity where Denmark, in Madison county, now stands. Here we came to a "three-notched" road, which had just been cut out, leading from Jackson to Brownsville. Taking the west end, running in the direction we were traveling, we arrived at the latter place in the afternoon of the following day. Brownsville had just been laid off and established as the county site of Haywood county. It contained not a dozen houses. The court-house and jail were being built of logs. Our place of destination was still some twenty odd miles further west, in the heart of the wilderness. My father, having provided himself with correct maps and surveys of the country, was enabled to work his way to the tract of land upon which he designed settling. Spring opening upon us, he was anxious to find the end of his road-making, and pushed on to find rest. Finding a newly-blazed way, showing now and then that wagon-wheels had gone over it, leading in the direction we were going, my father availed himself of it for the distance of seven or eight miles. Coming to a large creek, impassable without bridging at that season of the year, tents were pitched for an indefinite number of days. Every one that could use an ax, hatchet or hoe was called into requisition making roads and building bridges. Three pretty good-sized creeks and numerous branches intervened between our camp and the place of destination. The direction being north of west, the compass was non-available in finding the course. To obviate this difficulty, my father would ride ahead in the proper direction as far as the sound of his big horn could be heard, and blow, the negroes to be guided by the blowing of the horn, blazing the way until they came up to him. In this way he obtained quite a straight line to follow in cutting out the road. After many days of toil the road was cut, bridges made and hills dug down. Monday, of the second week in March, tents were struck and rolled up, never to be used again in traveling. That night we arrived on the bank of the beautiful creek mentioned in the opening of this chapter, making the trip in forty-eight days.

In a virgin land, teeming with nature's richest verdure, unknown to the ruthless tread of oppression, preserved for countless ages as the chosen hunting-ground of the red men, civilization had come to exercise dominion over it—to found its places of abode. Little did the pioneer settlers think that in less time than man's ordinary span of active life, the march of improvement, the progress of the age, would so soon cover its broad acres. It is not of the present that we would write, but of our country in its infant days, when the ax was a stranger in its giant forests; when the plow-share and the grubbing-hoe was first made bright and dull in preparing—in making it ready for enjoying civilized life—when its greatest need was man. The woods had already given signs of the opening of an early spring; the hickory was budding, and dogwood blossoms were whitening the forest—sure signs that the last frost had made its appearance. Dependent for "the staff of life" upon the growing of a crop of corn, everything was under strain to get through building and go to *clearing*. My father had selected his building site on a high level, or bench, fronting on the bluff, under which was the noted "Bluff Spring;" the land to the south and west slightly undulating, heavily wooded with poplar, black walnut, ash, oak and hickory. Before the end of the month we were all comfortably housed in a double log-house (of course), front gallery, with shed-room behind; the garden spot selected, cleared, grubbed (grubbing was the hardest work, the spot being a hazle-nut thicket) and planted, and all hands in the *new ground.* By the 1st of June eighty acres were cleared, under fence and planted in corn, with a small patch of cotton for domestic use. The garden teeming with every variety of early vegetables, the woods overrun with wild pea-vines (the delight of the cow), we had milk and butter in abundance, with good hog prospect. But the hogs—the greatest trouble was to keep the bear off them; they required to be constantly watched during the day, and driven up at night. I remember an occurrence that happened one day, while we were all in the *new ground*, chopping, cleaning up, and burning brush, worthy to be related as a *bear-hog* story. The hogs were driven out in the new ground, where the hands were at work, that an eye could be kept upon them. Late in the afternoon, when the clear ring of the ax, and the crackling fire, looming up from the brush-heap, was attracting every one's attention, we were startled by the sharp squeal of a hog, not more than one hundred yards off. The cry arose from many voices, "The bear—the bear has got a hog; it's the old big sow. I know her squeal—call the dogs. Here, Dash, here! Here, Sound, here, here! Send for master, with his long gun." In the meantime Jim, an athletic negro man, ran with all his might to her relief (it was the old big sow, sure enough, a huge sow with saddle-skirt ears) with his ax. So intent was bruin in securing his bacon that he did not heed the coming up of the negro man, who, intent upon dealing a death-lick, approached within easy striking distance. With ax raised high in air he let drive—his foot slipped—sprawling he went, his ax grazing the bear's head. Bruin, infuriated, mounted Cuffy, sprawling him his full length upon the ground. Men, women and children screamed for help. Help was, luckily, just in time. The dogs were up, and engaged the black monster's attention, pinching him behind every time he would put his head down to bite Jim, until my father came up with his long single-barrel. Approaching as close as possible, fearing a stray shot might find its home in one of his favorite dogs, he reached within a few feet. The dogs, being encouraged, made a furious attack, pressing the bear to a rout, when he rushed, with an angry growl, wide and extended jaws, toward my father, until he reached the muzzle of the long single-barrel. Thrusting it down his broad throat, he fired. Old Bruin sunk upon his knees, to rise no more. The long single-barrel was a notable "London fowling-piece." My father had brought it from North Carolina, from whence he moved to the old-settled portion of Mississippi. It was seven feet long. Twenty-four "blue whistlers" was an ordinary "buck load," and two ounces of small shot for a duck load. It was a common occurrence, when fired into a drove of deer, to "bring down" three or four. Deer were so plentiful that, in riding through the woods, it was rare to be out of sight of one. During the winter and early spring it was common to see as many as thirty and forty in one herd. In the spring they fed principally on the young buds. They would frequent at night the "new-ground" to feed upon the tender buds of the small growth which had been cut down during the day. "Fire-hunting" became a favorite, as well as an easy, mode of hunting. I remember, one dark, cloudy night, "we boys" had gone to bed, my father hallooed up Jack from his "quarters" to fix his pan and make ready for a fine hunt on the "new-ground." "We boys" were up and dressed in a jiffy, not surprised, however, that we could n't go, but to be up and wait the result of the hunt until the big gun fired, was all we wanted. Off stalked Jack, with the fire-pan upon his shoulder, my father trailing close behind him, with his long single-barrel, "we boys" following to the front steps (the entrance to the broad lawn in front of the house was over steps made of square hewed logs), where we took our seats—(I might as well say here that there were five of "we boys," two older and two younger than the writer)—watching in breathless silence the windings of the fire-pan through the new-ground. "There," says the oldest brother, "they have found eyes. See Jack moving his pan, so as to give father a good sight." The words were hardly uttered when, *bang!* went the old long-gun. No longer restrained, we broke for the "fire-pan," tumbling over brush and poles, which for the most part covered the ground, the two younger brothers crying out, now and then, "Stop; please don't leave us; it's so dark we can't see." Coming up to where the fire was burning, upon a large stump, we found father and Jack dragging the deer together. He had killed four outright, and crippled or wounded others. The dogs, alive to what was going on, were there before we came up. Following the blood of the wounded, they soon came up to two more dead, which were dragged up to the others. Half a dozen deer at one shot seems incredible. Facts, however, are sometimes stranger than fiction. The deer were feeding upon the tender buds around a newly-made brush-heap, standing thick as sheep round a salt-log. Beside, a discharge of twenty-four "blue whistlers" into a herd of deer such as were then seen in the wilds of the Big Hatchie, and particularly when standing circled round a brush-heap, from such a gun, was but little short of the destructive projectiles from the "little more grape, Captain Bragg," against the Mexicans. The cart was sent for, and the six deer taken to the house. Venison was no rarity, however; only the number of *eyes* that were seen, and how thick they stood round the brush-heap, was discussed. We were all getting tired—particularly the negroes—of "blue jerk."

The reader must bear with me in our *personal history;* we have aught else yet to write about. We were yet in the wilderness—in a wilderness of game—deer, bear, now and then an elk, the wolf, the panther, wildcat and catamount, and all the various sorts of "varmints." We had no neighbors, and if we had had, there were no roads leading to their dwelling-places. There were not so many as a half dozen cotemporary settlers north of the Big Hatchie, in Tipton county, and the nearest was twelve miles off, by section lines. And we had not become acquainted. It was not until fall, when the hunting season opened, that we saw or held intercourse with red or white man. The county was yet visited by bands of Chickasaw hunters, every fall and winter. They still regarded it as their hunting ground. My narrative, therefore, must be, for the most part, wrought from the wildwoods and its innumerable tenants, in which much of our *personal* history must crop out. The general features of the country north of the Hatchie, except for its richness of soil, giant forests, impenetrable canebrakes, tare-blanket thickets, grape and bamboo jungles, and the wild pea-vine in spring and summer, so thickly matted—overrunning the undergrowth—as to impede travel on foot or horseback, presented nothing of topographical interest. The same may be said of the country extending to the mouth of the Ohio and Tennessee rivers. It had long been the favorite hunting-ground of the Chickasaws and pioneer settlers, who were, for the most part, men of the woods, and lived by the chase. Of such were Davy Crockett, and many like him.

CHAPTER II.

Early Settlers Forming Neighborhoods—Joe Seahorn and the Hog's Hide—Nancy and her Peril with the Panther—Panther Hunt—The Road to Covington—First Ferry in Tipton on the Hatchie—Dickens and his Taxes—Old Jack.

BURIED, as it were, in the wilderness, beyond the outskirts of busy civilized life, we lived in Quaker simplicity. The schoolmaster and the preacher had not yet arrived in the land—nothing around us to imbue the young mind with "a sense of the vanity of the world." Peers of the noblest of the land, we were a law unto ourselves, drawing philosophy from the shades of the wild woods and the profusion of wild flowers that decked the bosom of mother earth. Our father dignified labor by requiring that every one should put his "hand to the plow." The field and the *new ground* were the objects of interest. During the spring and summer months the settling of our *new home* went on swimmingly. The bear and the hogs gave the only trouble—was the only source of annoyance. Their voracious appetites for hog-meat often exceeded the vigils of the herdsman. Many were torn and shockingly lacerated before he, with his dog and gun, could get to their relief. It may be interesting to the reader to know the habits and mode of the bear in procuring food. They often exhibit more than *beastly* skill in that particular. Cautiously approaching the hog, under cover of thick underbrush, a large tree or log, they make their way until within reach, when, rearing up upon their hinder feet, and making a leap, the hog is safe within the folds of their strong arms. Sinking deep their broad jaws across the hog's back, close up to the shoulders, they go to work to gratify their greed, waiting not for the animal to die. The most timid of the wild beasts of the woods, yet, when they get a taste of the blood of their victim, they hold on like grim death, often contending fearlessly with man and dog for their prey. It is in summer alone that they feed on flesh, upon which they never grow fat. As soon as the mast begins to harden they quit the fields and hog-meat, and soon begin to fatten. It is a novel sight to see them feeding in the "lappin season." This begins in the early fall, before the acorns begin to fall to the ground. They climb up the tallest oaks of the forest, and with their great arms they gather the limbs together as a sheaf of wheat, holding on to them until stripped of their fruit. In this way they continue through the lap, until the tree is stripped of its acorns, or until he gets his fill. By early winter they become fat, in a good mast year, and house up for the balance of the winter in some secluded place, near water, only coming out when thirsty, until spring. With old bear-hunters, the time for them to unhouse themselves is when the dogwood begins to blossom; the she-bear brings out her young then. February is the month for their parturition.

Soft, golden, sunny September, when the forest is in the "sear and the yellow leaf," with her crimson sunsets and "gray morn," sure signs of the first frost, is the happy period of the hunter's life—when the deer will have shed their summer suit, and taken on his winter gray and blue; the antlers of the noble buck dropping their soft velvet covering, and becoming hard and white; the bear getting lazy from his surfeit of fat, and taking himself to the thick jungle for winter quarters; the wild turkies, in countless numbers, flocking from the ridges to the bottoms. The most inviting grounds on the green earth, to the hunter, was the Big Hatchie country, at the period when my father moved to it. We marvel not that the Chickasaws had chosen it as their favorite hunting-ground.

During the fall and winter new-comers began to find their way, and found settlements north and east of us, yet we were without neighbors, save a few squatters and occupants. The smoke from their cabins could be seen rising up through the dense forest in many directions. Our nearest squatter neighbor was old Mrs. Seahorn, her son Joe, and son-in-law Bill Barnes. Joe and Bill were noted for living well, without ever being known to work; they dressed well and rode fine horses, and were rarely found at home. Where they went, or what they brought away, concerned but few, as they were not hemmed in by inquisitive neighbors. Joe was no hunter; Bill, however, was a good bee-hunter. The wild-woods afforded an abundance of honey-giving flowers; beside, in the virgin freshness of the land, the honey-dew lay heavy upon the thick foliage during the spring months. With Bill Barnes, honey was his only staple commodity, and afforded the main support of the Seahorn family. For the want of vessels to put his honey in, he resorted to the digging of troughs in which to keep it. An occurrence soon happened that required him to pre-empt in some other section of the wild-woods. My father had been missing some of his fattening hogs at a period of the year when old Bruin did not feed upon flesh. Old Jack, who was the hog minder and defender, was put to look out for signs that would lead to solve the mystery of the missing hogs. He was not long in getting on the right track. Stalking through a thick hazlenut thicket near the squatters' cabin, his dog grabbed up from behind a large log, the skin of a hog. It proved, from the flesh-marks, to be the skin of one of the missing hogs. Cutting a pole, he hoisted it upon his shoulder and brought it home. The mystery of the missing hogs was solved. My father sent for Joe Seahorn, and required from him an explanation as to how the hide of one of his hogs came to be covered up in the leaves near his house. Seahorn vowed his want of knowledge and total ignorance in the matter, visiting imprecations upon old Jack's head, swearing that the old negro lied if he said that he found the hide near his house, and accused him of being the guilty party, and then laying it upon him, to throw suspicion off from himself and the other negroes. My father, however, was in no wise convinced of Seahorn's innocence. Negro testimony being of no avail, he made him to understand that he must find an occupant claim in some other quarter, more *congenial* to the occupation he proposed following. Seahorn's hog-stealing soon found a place in song. Some of the boys worked off several verses, which was sung to the tune of "Harper's Creek and Roaring River." The following four lines are yet remembered of it, as it was sung in the neighborhood, by the boys and negroes:

"Joe Seahorn, he stol'd a hog,
The hide he hid behind a log.
Old Jack's dog, he found the hide,
And Seahorn swore that Jack he lied."

Early on the following morning, old Mrs. Seahorn came over to see my mother, to get her to "speak to the 'Squire," as she said, "not to be hard on my boy Josey." By way of a peace-offering, she brought an apron-full of "nice dried peaches," which she had cut and dried with her own hands; "and," says she, "here is some nice, new honey. I told the boys, last spring, when they showed my boy Pinkey where the white mare was, that when Bill Barnes cut a bee tree, I would give them a fill of honey; so here it is. I just brought it along in this gourd; it's my milk gourd; it's very nice." Then she appealed to my mother to talk to the 'Squire, and get him not to be hard on Josey. "And," says she, "we ain't going to stay here long, so I brought you some of the best peach-seed you ever did see; they's as yellew as gold, big as your two fists, and, when ripe, you can sock your thumb in them plumb to the seed; they is cling-stones. I just thought," said she,

"I would bring you them as a friendly offering, and something for you all to remember me by, for you all has been mighty kind to we all. Nancy was so sorry she didn't have something to send the 'Squire. She talks so much about his saving her from being eaten up by the panther. We all love the 'Squire for his kind act in saving Nancy's life from the jaws of the ugly beast. Do, pray, speak to the 'Squire not to be hard on Josey." My mother gave her a little coffee, which she tied up in the corner of her apron. With many thanks she bid her good-morning, saying, "Please do speak to the 'Squire not to be hard on Josey." The circumstance of my father's having saved little Nancy from a shocking death, occurred in this wise: The squatter's cabin was a short distance above the bluff spring, near the creek; they got their drinking water out of a "wet-weather spring," which, in dry weather, went dry. When they had to resort to the bluff spring for drinking water, one afternoon, late in the fall, little Nancy had been sent to the bluff spring. The path leading from the squatter's cabin meandered down a deep ravine to where it empted in the creek, and thence down to the spring. The little girl had over-staid her time at the spring; the shades of evening were fast upon her. When she started back, tripping along until she reached the mouth of the ravine, where the path turned through a dark jungle of undergrowth and over-hanging vines, a huge panther sprang upon her. My father happened to be on the hill above, where a couple of negro men were at work on some mill timbers. Hearing the *scream* of little Nancy, whom he had seen leaving the spring with her gourd of water, he immediately comprehended that something terrible had befallen her. The child's scream and wail increased and was heart-rending. He made for her with the utmost haste. The two negro men followed. Luckily, he had his short, large-bore rifle with him. Reaching the mouth of the ravinè, the scream of the child came from across the creek. He noticed the big gourd the little girl was carrying, at the mouth of the ravine, and quickly comprehended the peril she was in. He ran across the creek (the water was shallow), and upon reaching the top of the bank, he discovered a large panther, just entering the thick cane, fast hold of little Nancy, in the act of dragging her over a large log. The panther had just mounted the log, holding on to Nancy by the arm close up to her shoulder. Showing his broad side, quick as thought, a well-aimed bullet was sent through his heart. At the crack of the rifle, the panther sunk upon the log quivering in death. The two negro men were at my father's back when he fired, running up with their axes (seeing that the monster still held on to the little girl's arm), to give him the final blow. The panther was dead, yet her great jaws were fast hold of Nancy's arm, and had to be prized open to relieve her. Her little arm was shockingly larcerated and torn; otherwise, save some slight scratches, she was unhurt. It was a she panther, and her aim was to drag the child alive to her den, where she had her young. The men cut a grape vine, noosed it around the panther's neck, and dragged it home, while my father took little Nancy in charge to her mother. It was for thus rescuing little Nancy from the jaws of death that old Mrs. Seahorn had expressed herself so grateful. Hardly had they gotten across the creek, when, in the thick cane behind them, rang, with the wild shrieks and yells of a panther, the mate of the old she just killed. He had doubtless been standing guard to the young cubs, sharpening his teeth upon hearing the screams of the child, and ready for the slaughter. His disappointment, and absence of his companion, had brought forth his terrific yells.

My father decided that night to give the old gentleman panther a warming the next morning. He was certain to be found near the den, watching over the cubs, and waiting the return of their dam. Every arrangement was made for the hunt. My two eldest brothers had killed their deer. The next to the oldest had become an expert hunter. Life in the woods, with rifle in hand, he greatly preferred to the "plow handles." He was a splendid shot with all, never failing to bring down his gobbler at long range. The old long, single barrel, the short, large bore (called a Yorger), and the little rifle, running sixty bullets to the pound, were all the guns my father had. Old Jack, who generally formed one of the party in a hunt, and who was a pretty good shot, was sent over to Mrs. Seahorn's to borrow Bill Barnes' rifle. (Joe and Bill Barnes were absent at the time.) By sun-up we were all across the creek (I was permitted to go along to see the young cubs as well as the fun). Reaching the log upon which the old she was killed the evening before, the dogs dashed off on a running trail in the direction she was aiming to drag her prey. To pursue with rapidity was impossible; the thick cane and jungle was, for the most part, impenetrable, and but for the openings caused by the rotting out of the fallen trees, it would have been impossible for man to have gotten through it. "Hark! hark!" says my father, "*the dogs have come to a bay;* keep a sharp look out boys." The sharp, angry bark of the dogs impelled the hunters forward as rapidly as they could go. Getting close up, warning was given to "keep a sharp look out." Soon we came upon them surrounding a large "clay-root," their hair erect, barking most fiercely. "List! list!! boys, the old fellow is crouched some where near; keep a sharp look out." Just then old Jack had gotten within a few feet of the clay-root; when my father noticed it, from the crouched position of one of the dogs, and his fierce gaze through the opening of the cane overhead, he called to him, "Look out, Bull sees him." Simultaneously with the quick spoken words of warning to old Jack, came the sharp crack of the little rifle, and with it the sprawl of Jack, and the panther upon him. In an instant the dogs covered both Jack and the panther. The moment was terrific and painful, until the negro began to crawl out from under the dead monster. The next to the eldest brother, quickly comprehending the situation, in his eagerness to get the first shot, had slipped around to the body of the large fallen tree, where he could get a full view of the "clay-root," which rose above the bending cane, discovering the panther crouched upon a large root, intently watching the movements of the dogs below. Quick as thought, his rifle was well-aimed and fired, sending his bullet through his heart; in his death leap, he sprang upon Jack. He was the monster panther of the woods; his full length stretched out upon the ground, was eleven feet two inches from the tip of his nose to the end of his tail. The entrance to the den of the old she was under the *clay-root*, in the hollow of the fallen tree, large enough for the dogs to enter and pass in for many feet. The cubs had got into the hollow beyond their reach Dry sticks and faggots were procured, a fire built up in the entrance of the den, and the cubs left to their fate.

My father, the fall of the first year he settled in the wilderness, surveyed out and cut a road through the Hatchie bottom, and established the first ferry on the Hatchie, below McGuire's, in Haywood. There was then a continuous road from Brownsville to Covington, and became the principal road of travel between the two places, and my father's house the only habitation on the road, which of necessity became a "house of entertainment." The most frequent travel was by exploring parties, looking after and locating land for future settlement.

An amusing incident occurred soon after my father commenced *taking in travelers*, which may find interest with the reader. Some half dozen well dressed gentlemen rode up one night, while the family were at supper, and asked to "stay all night." They were ushered in the best room, where a blazing fire was burning. It was winter, and the night cold. Supper was ordered for "six hungry men," who hadn't "eat a mouthful since early morn." Word was soon conveyed to my mother that they were real, nice, broadcloth gentlemen. Of course, something extra nice was in rapid course of preparation. The servants and everybody spread themselves. The children, you know, couldn't be kept out of sight; they were bound to *see* the fine strangers. New jackets and clean white aprons were put on, and the servants required to put on clean frocks. My mother got out her best *damask*. The new *tea tray* and *china* were brought into requisition. Preserves, in *glass dishes*, were arranged upon the table. A fresh cake of butter was fixed up most tastily, in "pine apple shape," and graced the center of the table, and the last two *sperm* candles, stuck in the tall silver candle-sticks, were lighted, and the guests invited in to supper. My mother, with her new "turban" on, had taken her seat at the head of the table, behind the new tea-tray and glittering service. The party entering the *dining-room* (a shed room boarded up with clapboards) were led by a tall and stately silver-haired gentleman. Advancing to the chair assigned him, he paused, resting his hand upon the back, with a fixed gaze at my mother, whose eyes were also riveted upon him. A mutual recognition followed, he advancing as she rose to meet him. Her features expressing a pleasant surprise, she exclaimed, "Colonel William Polk, of North Carolina!" and extended her hand. "And this is *Mrs. Patsy Seawell* ———," said the Colonel, clasping her hand in both of his. "My dear madam, this is the most joyous meeting since I left our native State." My father, who had stepped out to give some orders about their horses, stepped in just then, and, recognizing each other, a general introduction went the rounds.

Colonel William Polk (father of the late Right Reverend Bishop Polk) and my mother were familiarly acquainted in their young days. Their meeting was most unexpected to both of them. He, with a party of young men, were exploring the country and looking after their landed interests. With the party was young Dickens, son of Colonel Dickens, of Madison. His business seemed to be to pay the taxes on the large landed interests of his father, and possibly to make further investments in lands. With less mother wit than good looks and fine clothes, he talked much of a roll of United States bills he carried about his person, which he called his "taxes." A young Seawell, son of the late Judge Seawell, of Raleigh, North Carolina, was of the party. Seawell was a great tease, and wonderfully fond of a good joke. Young Dickens was the butt of the party, easily quizzed, and afforded great merriment. Whenever the conversation would relax, Seawell or some member of the party would ask him to feel for his "taxes." He would run his hand around under his vest and announce that "they were all safe." To sleep the party it was necessary to have "pallets" made down on the floor of the best room. Young Dickens was the first to lay down. Taking off his coat and vest, he stretched himself out on his pallet, while his companions remained up cracking jokes. He soon fell asleep, when Seawell suggested a practical joke upon the innocent sleeper, who, in turning over upon his side, exposed to view the red morocco belt containing his "taxes." The belt was cautiously taken from around his body. Dickens *snored away*, and the rest of the party retired for the night. Dickens was the first to rise in the morning. Finding a *rousing* fire burning in the broad fire-place, he bounced up from his pallet. His first care was to feel for his "taxes." The belt was gone. He cried aloud, "My taxes! My taxes! By thunder, where is my taxes?" With one leap he was at the door, holding on to old Jack's coat-tail. Jack had just finished making the fire, and was leaving the room, with the gentlemen's boots under his arm. Young Dickens jerked him back in the room and commenced a search in his pockets for his money-belt, crying out in a wailing voice, "My taxes! My taxes!" Jack protested and declared that he didn't have them, until he began to get a little worried, when he said: "De Lord bless me, *mister*, dis nigger don't know nothin' 'bout your *tacks*. What you think he wants wid *your tacks!* Bless me, mister, master's got plenty tacks!" "You old fool," said Dickens, "I don't mean tacks—taxes! money, in a red morocco belt I buckled around me when I went to bed last night. When I got up this morning, it was gone. Nobody has been in this room but you." "Oh! aha! Money, you say; money in red morocco belt! No, sir! Dis nigger knows nothin' bout it. You got hold de wrong nigger dis time; dat you have." In the mean time the whole party were awake, and enjoying the scene before them. Dickens, not finding his taxes upon the person of Jack, and becoming *overpowered* with a sense of his loss, sunk down in the nearest chair and boo-hooed outright. Seawell's sympathies were touched. He arose from an adjoining bed, picking up the counterpane off' of the pallet Dickens had slept on. He gave it a shake, and out fell the *red morocco belt.* The young man sprang to it. Picking it up, he burst out into a half laugh and cry of joy, saying, "What a fool I was." Jack returned soon with the gentleman's boots. Dickens said to him that he was only joking, pitching him a silver half dollar. "Thankee, thankee! This'll buy me more'n tacks enough to make me two pairs of shoes."

CHAPTER III.

Neighborhoods Forming—Thomas Durham, Founder of Durhamville—Johnny Bradford—Thomas Thompson, Esq.—D. C. Russell—The First Frame House—Jacob Niswanger—William Murphey, the Hatter, and his Black Snakes—Joseph Wardlow—Stephen Childress—Thomas Childress—William Turner and Parson Collins—Their First Night in the Big Hatchie Country—Arthur Davis, the Pioneer Preacher—First School-house in Tipton North of Hatchie—Old Man Larkin Gaines, the First Schoolmaster.

THE succeeding and following year witnessed the rapid settling up of the country north and north-east of us. Neighborhoods had begun to form; the schoolmaster and the preacher had found their way in the land. Thomas Durham, who was our first *militia Colonel* in Tipton, north of Hatchie, founded a settlement on the high hill, where the village of Durhamville, which took his name, now stands. Honest Johnny Bradford found his way from Illinois, and settled below Durham's, on the head waters of Williams' creek, where he spent his last and best days.

Thomas Thompson and the Russells moved in from North Carolina, and settled on the waters of Fisher's and Garner's creeks, and became the nucleus of the settlement north of Williams' creek. David C. Russell had built the first framed house in

Tipton north of Hatchie; it was built in 1827 by the two young Adams, who came to the settlement with William Turner and Parson Collins. The two young men (brothers) sawed out with a whipsaw the lumber with which they built the house—the whipsaw, for many years, supplied all the lumber that was used. The Gillilands came in from Pennsylvania a few years after, and purchased the house of Russell, and built a mill on what was then called Fisher's creek, which afterwards was called Gilliland's creek, by which name it is yet known. They established the first store of any note in Tipton north of Hatchie; men of enterprise and business tact, they established the first store on "Hurricane Hill," and contributed largely to the interest and prosperity of the neighborhood.

Thomas Thompson was the first magistrate in Tipton north of Hatchie, and a member of the County Court for many years. A worthy and most excellent good citizen, he ever maintained the dignity and high respect due his court, by which he was enabled to command the respect and aid of all good citizens in quelling an outbreak, which rarely failed to occur on all public occasions.

The writer remembers to have heard related an amusing account of the way the law was executed in those days. The 'Squire usually held his courts on Saturdays. At the same time and place it was usual for the settlement to arrange for a "shooting-match." While his court was in session, a fight grew up between Joe Seahorn and another neighbor. The 'Squire ordered that the offending parties be brought before him. Seahorn, who was guilty of the assault and battery, took to his heels, when he saw the officer coming; finding that he would be overtaken, he took a tree, and up it he went to the top. The officer commanded that he come down; he defiantly refused, and dared the officer to "come up and take him." Thinking himself safe, he crowed like a cock upon his tallest perch. The officer, resolute and fertile of expedients, sent for an axe—one was close at hand—with which he went to work to cut him down. When the tree began to crack and show signs of falling, Joe began to think the matter getting serious, and hallooed out to "hold on," that he "surrendered," that he would come down. The officer hallooed back for him to "hold on," that the tree would soon be down, and whacked away. Joe could stand it no longer. When the tree began to crack and shake, down he slid, striking the ground as the tree left the stump. The officer, with his *posse*, seized him, and marched him up before the 'Squire, who ordered that he be held in close confinement until the shooting-match was over. The officer, wishing to take his chance at shooting for a quarter of beef, and there being no strong place at hand in which to confine the prisoner, sought a cart body which lay convenient, and put him under it, and with the aid of the bystanders, brought a heavy log and weighted it down; thus Joe was kept closely caged until the shooting-match was over. The other party was let off with an apology on his part, and a reprimand from the court.

Cotemporary with the settlements on Williams' and Fisher's creeks, Captain Stephen Childress settled in the thick woods six or more miles below, on a creek, which took his name, where he opened a large plantation. The Captain lived but a few years. His widow, who was the sister of Thomas H. and Jesse Benton, with a large family, survived him many years. Thomas Childress, son of Captain Stephen, with his beautiful young wife, settled in the woods near his father's the same year. He is yet living near where he first settled, and is, I believe, the only surviving Childress of the old stock. He yet maintains, under the weight of many years, an elastic step and the dignity of his race.

The year following, old man Jacob Niswanger, and his son-in-law, Joseph Wardlow, moved in from South Carolina, and opened up a large plantation on Garner's creek. The same year, and from the same State, came old man Larkin Gaines, and his sons, Pendleton, Powell and Abner. Few "new-comers" contributed more to the interest and advancement of the settlement, than Niswanger and Waldron. The old man Jacob, a man of many eccentricities of character, was a genius with all. Everything needed or useful in the economic management of his affairs bore marks of his handy-work. By his probity and industry he amassed a fortune. A hatter by trade, he kept up his shop as long as he lived. He brought old man Murphey with him from South Carolina, who was long noted for being the best maker of hats in West Tennessee.

William Murphey had his idiosyncrasies. Those of us who knew him when we were boys yet remember him and his black snakes with an amusing interest. The only instance known of the snake's being cultivated and utilized is perhaps due to William Murphey, the hatter. He found them better *mousers* than the house cat, and introduced them into his shop for the protection of his furs and newly made hats. On a warm sunshiny day, you would see them coiled up in every crack and nitch in his shop, with their black eyes glistening like so many newly opened chinquepins. They kept his shop free of rats and mice. It is human to be afraid of snakes. They answered him a good purpose in keeping away the meddlesome boys. An amusing as well as a thrilling incident occurred to the old gentleman soon after he arrived in the settlement. He had strolled out one day in the "new ground" on a snake hunt. He soon scared up, in the thick brush, a monster black snake, and made for it. The snake being pressed hard for a hiding place, took to a hole in the end of a hollow pole. He carefully stopped up the entrance to the hollow, and shouldering it, he started for the shop. He had gone but a short distance, when he began to experience a choking sensation; the snake had found his way out at another hole, and thrown himself around the old hatter's neck. It being a large and powerful snake, he was unable to extricate himself. With difficulty he was able to call for help. Luckily several negro men were at work close by, who, discovering the perilous fix the old man was in, ran to his relief. It was only with their knives that they could prevent *strangulation*, by cutting the monster loose. The old gentleman was very thankful for the timely help, but sorely regretted to lose so fine a rat-catcher.

Joseph Wardlow built his first house at the big spring, forming the head of Garner's creek, and afterward made his permanent settlement below his father-in-law's, near the same creek, where he resided until the county of Lauderdale was formed in 1836, when he fixed his residence at Ripley, the newly located county site, building the first house in the place. He continued his residence in Ripley until his death, which occurred in 1863, in the seventieth year of his age. His name, long intimately connected and associated with the rise and progress of Lauderdale, as among the fathers of the county, is perpetuated in his noble sons, who, of the present day, stand among its most worthy and prominent citizens.

The Fishers, Blackwells, Doctor Abner Phillips, and others worthy of mention, were cotemporary in the Thompson-Russell settlement.

The settlement to the east and south of Durhamville was formed by Matthew Pickett, Johnny Stone, William Turner, Kent Penic, Estes and others, many of whose decendants yet cultivate the land, and reside on the homes of their fathers.

Among those of the pioneer and early immigrant settlers, whose long and useful life is yet spared to recount the perils and hardships of pioneer life in the Big Hatchie country, none is more worthy a page in these semi-historic reminiscences than William Turner—Uncle Billy, as he is familiarly and reverentially called—who, in the spring-time of manhood, with his young and newly married wife, in company with several of his neighbors, cut loose their moorings from the shores of their native land, Kentucky, and floated out the Barron river into the Green, and down the Ohio into the Mississippi, landing at the mouth of the Big Hatchie, in the month of February, in the year 1827, in search of a home in a wild, and, to him, an unknown land.

His companions were Parson Reson B. Collins, Charles Cullin, and two young men named Adams. Heading the prow of their keel, with all their earthly goods, up the Hatchie, they poled away until they reached a point of high land interesting to look at. Dividing in search of a place upon which to locate, two took to the woods north of the river, and two south, the fifth remaining with the "women folks" on the boat.

Billy Turner and Parson Collins took to the north side, and struck out for the hills, and soon become lost in the woods. Bogueing about all day, they found themselves, at nightfall, on a high bluff, overlooking the tops of the tall trees to the north and west. They stood upon the Cole creek bluffs, ten or more miles away from their boat, bewildered in a wilderness of wild beasts. They brought a halt to gather in their confused thoughts. Turner proposed that they strike a fire and wait till morning. The Parson opposed it, expressing his fears that they would be eaten up during the night by wild beasts. The brave-hearted Turner went to work, however, and gathered dry wood, built a fire and resolved to spend the night. Tired, and without food, he rolled himself up upon the ground to sleep. Hardly had he fallen to sleep, when the Parson aroused him, saying that he could hear "the tramp of the wild beasts;" that he could hear them "snapping and sharpening their teeth;" that they would be "eaten up alive before morning;" that he must get up and they would "watch together."

Billy, thinking that he ought to pray as well as watch, turned over and dropped to sleep again. He was again aroused from his slumbers by the Parson saying that he was dying of thirst; that if he didn't get some water soon he would die. What to do, or where to find water for his frightened, feverished companion, was a puzzle. Something had to be done, however, or he would die of fright and thirst. So he got up and commenced looking about for water; none could be found, unless it be under the bluff, which it seemed impossible to reach. To save life, however, they commenced sliding down, holding on to such twigs and rough places as they could feel; they were in utter darkness. Down they went, however, the Parson ahead, until they struck the bank of the creek. But how should he get to the water? The bank was perpendicular. The cane stood thick and heavy upon the bank, bending over to the surface of the water. The only way to get to the water was to slide down on the cane. So down the Parson crawled on top of the bending cane until his burning face came in contact with the cold water. Reviving from his fright, and slaking his thirst, his trouble was to get back from his perilous situation, which he had just began to realize. His friend Billy could render him no assistance, nor could he see him, with his heels cocked up in the air, and his head touching the water, for the black darkness that reigned under the bluff. After many efforts and almost superhuman exertion, the Parson succeeded in reversing his position, and getting his head up, he pulled himself to shore. They got back to the fire again—how, the narrator says, was impossible to tell. It was thus they spent their first night in the Big Hatchie country.

When the morning came, they were at a loss to know which direction to take to get back to the boat. From the high bluff the Parson heard a chicken crow. He became almost crazed with delight, and told Billy that it was his rooster on the boat. Taking out his pocket-compass, he took the course. After several hours travel, they reached the boat, satisfied with the Cole creek hills. Cullen and one of the Adams boys had come in from their exploration on the south side, and reported unfavorably.

They went to work and poled higher up, reaching Childress' landing, where they made fast, and blazed their way up to the Thompson and Russell settlement. The year after "Uncle Billy" moved over and settled on Camp creek; a favorite camping creek with the Chickasaws, and from which circumstance it took its name. For many years he enjoyed himself with the Indians, when they would come in on their fall hunts. He has told the writer, that he has counted as many as thirty deer, brought to their camp of a morning before the frost had left the ground. He still resides where he first made his permanent settlement in Tipton, now Lauderdale, forty-five years ago. Few men have lived so long and blameless a life as Uncle Billy Turner; noted for his many Christian virtues, he is venerated and esteemed by the community in which he lives, and highly respected by all who know him.

As a pioneer preacher, Parson Reson B. Collins proved himself unequal to the task. After a severe spell of fever, his mind lost its balance, and his friends prevailed on him to move back to Kentucky, which he did, after remaining a couple of years.

The man for the times, and suited to the work, soon made his appearanee in the land, in the person of Arthur Davis, who, lacking nothing in moral worth, or physical courage, came with the broad banner of his Master's kingdom in one hand, and the broad sword in the other. He came preaching that the wolf shall dwell with the lamb—that the "weaned child shall put his hand on the cockatrice's den"—that man was born to a "higher and brighter civilization." Few men knew better how to take the "bull by the horns," or win to his Master's kingdom a sinner's soul. Fond of pioneer life, he gloried in being called to preach in the wilderness. The writer is indebted to an old friend of Reverend Mr. Davis for many thrilling incidents, illustrative of the moral and physical heroism of the man. In the early settlement of the country, and before the building of churches, even with round logs, Mr. Davis made an appointment that he would preach at a certain school-house, on a certain day, in the vicinity of Denmark. A band of *outlaws*, living in the settlement, seeing the notice sticking up in the neighborhood, give it out that "no d—d Methodist preacher should preach in that house," and if Mr. D. attempted to fill his appointment, they would give him a sound drubbing. When he came to fill his appointment, he was informed of the threats, and advised that his life would be in danger if he undertook to preach. He paid no attention to their fears, and heeded not their advice, but went to his appointment. On reaching the place, he found the log-house already filled with the anxious and curious of the neighborhood, and the regulators standing apart with their sticks and clubs. He passed in, and up to the place assigned as a temporary pulpit. Inclining his head as a mark of respect to the congregation, he paused and surveyed, with a penetratiug eye, every member of the assembled neighborhood. Not a man of them did he know. He opened service, took his text, and preached. After the service was over, he announced an appointment, "Providence permitting," to preach at the same place again, on a stated day named, and invited the congregation to attend him out in the grove.

He passed out, as he went in, without turning his head to the right or to the left, and stopped at a stump. Taking off his hat and coat he laid them upon the stump, and then, turning to the assembled neighborhood, asked if there was present a member of any church, and paused for a reply. A gentleman stepped forward and replied that he had been a member of the Presbyterian church. "That will do, sir; thank you," said Mr. Davis. "I have a wife and one child. Her name is Drucilla. She lives at a certain place"—here giving such directions that he could not fail to find her. "I want you to promise, by the vow you took when you joined the church, that if anything should happen to Arthur Davis to-day, by which he should never see her again, that you will tell her how it happened, and all about it. Now, Mr. Regulators," turning to a clump of men who were standing apart from the crowd, "I am ready for you. Come one at a time, and I'll show you who Art. Davis is." They looked at one another, and then at the preacher. "Don't keep me waiting," says he. "You have made your threats that no d—d Methodist preacher should preach in that house," pointing to it. "I am a Methodist preacher, and I have preached in it, according to my appointment. I am now ready to meet you, according to your appointment, one at a time, and you will make the acquaintance of Art. Davis."

The leader of the band threw down his club, walked up to the brave-hearted Davis and offered him his hand saying: "Mr. Davis, you are my sort of man; I like you, sir; you shall preach here whenever it may please you to do so, and I will see you do it in peace. You are the preacher for me."

With that the neighborhood gathered around him, introducing one another, until he had made the personal acquaintance of every one present. He was ever after that a welcome preacher in the neighborhood.

Not long after that, a camp-meeting was being held near Denmark. Mr. Davis was, with other preachers, in attendance. It was a custom, in the early days of camp-meetings held in the Big Hatchie country, to organize a police to preserve order on the ground, and to keep out stragglers. During the progress of the meeting a half dozen or more rowdies and desperadoes, being instigated by a wild spirit and bad whisky, got up a fuss, which threatened to break up the meeting. The police, or guard, as they were then called, succeeded in arresting all of the disturbers, save one, who defied the guard and the whole camp-meeting. He had backed himself in between two tents, and he was protected in the rear by another tent. The passage-way to him was just wide enough for one man to pass in. There the desperado had taken refuge, brandishing his bowie-knife, and threatening death to any one who dared put his hands upon him. Mr. Davis, hearing of the difficulty, quietly remarked that he would go and take him. Approaching the crowd which had assembled in front of the desperate man with his bowie-knife, he at once comprehended the work to be done. Reaching the entrance to the passage-way in which the desperado stood, with his glistening blade in hand, he turned to the by-standers and asked that they would make him two promises, to which they assented. "Then," says he, "you will promise me, first, if I am killed, that you will see that my wife Drucilla and the children are cared for; and you will promise me, second, that you will hang that devil," pointing to the desperado, "upon yon limb," pointing up to a suitable limb for the purpose. Turning to the outlaw he quietly said: "Now, sir, you are my prisoner." No sooner did he make the first firm step toward him than the outlaw threw down his knife, advanced, and meeting him, said: "Parson Davis, you are the only man alive that can take me. I am your prisoner." The meeting progressed without further disturbance.

Few men possessed the personal courage of Mr. Davis. His earnest and firm personal bearing was as an array of sharp steel, when directed towards an offender. The power of his moral influence over the wicked was marked with equal success. The boldness with which he asserted his right to talk to sinners was happily illustrated at a camp-meeting held near Brownsville. The good work was going on swimmingly; the mourner's bench was filled, and gave promise of the conversion of many souls. Mr. Davis, in passing along, administering to their troubled souls, came to an old and hardened sinner, a gentleman of his acquaintance. He saw that he was "under conviction." Laying his heavy hand upon his shoulder, he said, in a loud and strong voice: "Pray! pray hard; pray with all your mind, might and soul. You are a moving, breathing mass of putrefaction. Pray with all your mind and strength, for you are the very butt-cut of sin." The power and force of his language struck the old sinner with such terror as to his situation that he slid from the bench into the straw, and wrestled with the devil until he triumped. Such was the power and force of character of the best pioneer preacher that ever filled an appointment in the Big Hatchie country.

The first school-house in Tipton, north of Hatchie, was built in 1827, in the Thompson settlement, and old man Larkin Gaines was the first schoolmaster. The writer, with Dr. Jacob N. Wardlow, now the Clerk and Master of the Chancery Court of Lauderdale, and Sam. A. Thompson, Esq., the present Chairman of the County Court of Lauderdale, were among his first pupils.

CHAPTER IV.

John C. Barnes, the Pioneer Blacksmith—What Became of General Tipton's Jack—The Chickasaws and the Shooting Match—The First Tub Mill and Cotton Gin—Joshua Farrington, the Gin Maker—Temple, the Screw Cutter and Model Bear Hunter—Bolivar Merchants—Pitser Miller—The Author's First Killing.

JOHN C. BARNES was the pioneer blacksmith in Tipton, north of Hatchie. His shop was on the waters of Fisher's creek. Barnes was a good citizen, though a bachelor, and had the advancement and prosperity of the settlement very much at heart. Of robust constitution, he stood six feet two in his stocking feet, broad across the chest, with shoulders and arms of a Vulcan, and was a skillful and most reliable workman with all.

The bringing into cultivation of the rich new lands began to require more work stock than were brought in by the settlers. Barnes, wishing to contribute his share toward *increasing* the stock of the land, proposed bringing a jack into the settlement and establish his headquarters at his blacksmith shop. His proposition was approbated by the neighborhood, with promises of patronage. But the grave question arose, first, as to where one could be had, and secondly, the money required to pay for one. A good jack in those days was worth from six to eight hundred dollars, which was more money than

Barnes, backed by the *settlement*, could conveniently raise. My father, hearing of Barnes' enterprise, and equally anxious with the lower settlement, to begin the raising of mules, sent for him. Barnes, full of hope-giving promise, with the message he had received, was at my father's to breakfast the next morning. He and my father talked over the subject-matter of his visit, which resulted in his going over to see General Tipton, residing south of the Hatchie, near Covington.

General Tipton was among the first settlers south of the Big Hatchie, in the county which bore his name. His place of dwelling was beautifully situated, four miles northeast of Covington, where he established a large plantation. He early introduced into the country the "best blooded stock." He took great interest in raising fine horses, mules and cattle, by which he became a great benefactor to the early settlers. Barnes, without delay, went over to see the General, and by an arrangement satisfactory to both parties, obtained his fine jack "Moses," and brought him over to his blacksmith shop. There being no printing offices yet in the country, Barnes repaired to old man Gaines, who taught a school in the settlement, and who wrote a fine, big hand, and got him to write off handbills, which he did, announcing, in a flowing big hand, that "General Tipton's celebrated Jack, 'Moses,' fifteen and a half hands high, would keep his headquarters for the season at Barnes blacksmith shop," etc. Sticking them up, one at the school-house, one at the meeting-house, and through the settlement generally, the neighbors flocked to the blacksmith shop to see General Tipton's famous jack "Moses," and Barnes felt that his fortune would be made in one *season*. His blacksmith work, in the meantime, kept him busy during spring and early summer, which, with the *standing* profits that promised to crop out of the "celebrated Moses," he passed the summer with golden dreams of a rich harvest from his enterprise.

The Chickasaws had not yet abandoned the Big Hatchie country as their favorite hunting-ground. Bands of hunters came in every fall, hunting in the Hatchie Bottom, until they loaded their ponies with deer, bear and other skins, which they took to Bolivar, a trading post for Indian traffic. Game of every description was so plentiful that the whites paid little or no attention to their coming or going. They were proverbially polite, friendly, and wholly inoffensive. To the nearest settlers they would bring in the finest haunches of venison, fat gobblers and bear meat. They hunted for the most part for the *peltries*, curing only as many venison hams as they could conveniently pack away on their ponies.

The hunting season had opened. Barnes, however, was no hunter. He was regarded as the rising man of the settlement, and began to think it was not good to be "alone in the world." A wedding was soon talked of at Captain Childress', some six miles below in the "thick woods." Barnes was spotted as the lucky man, and the Captain's eldest daughter as the woman. She was a widow. The wedding came off, and Barnes took his bride home. Arriving at home with his loving charge, he was met with the stern reality that "Moses" had gotten out and taken himself off to the "wilderness." All hands had gone to the wedding, and none could tell how he got out or whither he had gone. It was night, and nothing could be done until morning. Barnes rose early, and his first care was to find the whereabouts of the General's jack. Finding from his tracks that he had gone in the direction of the Hatchie Bottom, he returned to breakfast. After breakfast, he, with his foreman in the shop, went in search of "Moses." Taking his track, they followed it until they came to the thick switch-cane, where they could track him no farther. Bogueing about in the cane until night came upon them, they were compelled to return, having hunted all day in vain. A general search was made the next day, several of the neighbors joining in the hunt; but "Moses" had lost himself in the wilderness, where he could not be found. Barnes grew uneasy; he was troubled. Could he have been stolen? Hardly, for he had been tracked to the thick cane. The Chickasaws were in camp some eight miles above. None had been seen so low down, and if they had, no one thought for a moment that they were guilty of the theft. They had been coming in every hunting season, and were never known to trespass upon any one's rights. No, the Chickasaws had never been guilty of a wrong. In the meantime the winter rains set in early, overflowing all the streams. The Hatchie rose rapidly, inundating the bottom. "Moses" had not yet returned. The conclusion Barnes came to was, that he had been caught in the overflow and drowned. The winter passed, and Barnes had to report to the General the loss of his jack, acknowledging his responsibility in the premises. He promised to make good his value as soon as he was able to do so. The General, kind at heart and in sympathy with Barnes for his loss, was lenient. Barnes went to work in his shop, redoubling his energies. New-comers were rapidly settling around him. His shop work increased. He made and sharpened all the plows for eight or ten miles around. Happening to be on the river fishing one day, as a trading boat was descending, the Captain hailed him and inquired whether any *peltries* were on sale in his neighborhood. In the meantime the boat drifted around in the eddy where he was fishing, coming up broadside to the bank. The deck, or roof, of the boat was covered with skins of all kinds. It was sunny September, and the skins were being sunned and aired. A conversation grew up, Barnes asking the Captain what kind of skins he was buying, what he was paying, and the points he was trading to and from, when the Captain remarked that he had bought a hide of an animal at Bolivar novel in the *peltry trade.* The novelty was turned over, with the hair side up, a huge hide, with head, ears, and the eye holes well stretched. No sooner was Barnes' attention called to it when he exclaimed: "By thunder! Captain, it's my jackass's skin. 'Moses,' have I found you at last? Captain, where did you come across that hide?" The Captain told him that he purchased it with other skins from Bills & McNeal, of Bolivar. Barnes then related the story of the missing jack, and the Captain, being impressed with the truth of the statement, readily turned the hide over to Barnes, who took it home and put it away for safe keeping. The following month, October, the Chickasaws came in for their fall hunt. Barnes was on the lookout for them. They came down to the number of sixty or seventy, and camped at the mouth of Fisher's Creek, in the vicinity where "Moses" had lost himself the fall previous. They were very friendly. Barnes was favorably known to many of them. He had, on previous seasons, repaired their guns. Wholly ignorant of the grave charge awaiting them, several were soon out to the shop to have the locks of their guns fixed. Barnes had a talk with them. Learning that it was the same party that were in the bottom hunting the fall previous, he fell upon a strategy to get them out to his shop. Fixing their locks, he told them that a great "shooting-match" was going to take place at his shop next Saturday, then three days off, and invited them to come and bring all of their best shots; that they were going to shoot for the skin of a large and beautiful animal, the only one of the sort that was ever killed in the Hatchie Bottom. Delighted with the opportunity of shooting with the white man, and for such a prize skin, they left in great glee, promising to come and bring all of their best marksmen. Barnes was not long in communicating with his neighbors and arranging for the "shooting match." Saturday came. The best shots of the neighborhood, numbering thirty, had arrived. Soon the Indians came galloping up on their ponies, numbering between sixty and seventy.

The blacksmith shop was at the cross-roads, on a high, level bench of land, thickly shaded with large poplar, oak and hickory, free from undergrowth. A broad board had been charred, by holding it over a fire until it was black. The "bull's eye" was cut and pinned in the center of the "black-board," which was nailed breast high on a large poplar, and ninety yards stepped off. The Indians were to choose from among them five of their best shots, and the whites the same number. Judges were appointed to arrange the order of shooting. A silver half-dollar was cast up, "heads or tails," to decide which side should have the first shot. It was won by the red men. The judges announced everything ready for the shooting to begin. Four shots, in their order, was made, and the judges decided there was a "tie." The last round would decide. The red man squared himself to the mark, slowly bringing his rifle to his shoulder, and in breathless silence raised its long barrel until his sight covered the "bull's eye," and fired. *He drove the center.* It was the first shot that broke the cross (†). The Indians yelled with gleeful delight. The remaining shots were wide of the mark, and the Chickasaws whooped and yelled, calling for the prize skin. Barnes was ready with it. He deliberately walked out with the hide of "Moses" rolled up under his arm, and unrolled it upon the ground, to the astonished gaze of the red men. There was the hide of the celebrated jack, "Moses," with its mouse-colored hair and black streak running down its back, its flanks and belly white as cotton, relieved by the dark rings of the neck and head, with ears sticking up, and eye-holes circled with thick tufts of short white hair, spread out on the ground. The red men pressed up close to get a sight. The winner of the prize gathered it up, to exhibit it, as well as to examine it more closely. Turning it over, he broke out with a jolly, semi-savage "Ha! ha! ha! Me kill him. Me shoot him. See my bullet hole! [running his finger through the fatal hole.] Ha! ha! Me sell him to Bolivar. Me get him again. Ha! ha!" Old man Fullen—Ben Fullen, proprietor of "Fullen Ferry"—who was not in the secret of Barnes' strategy, exclaimed aloud, that it was "the hide of General Tipton's jack;" he would "swear by the *flesh marks* that it was. See them eye-holes, and them rings round his big ears!" "Hush!" said Barnes, "let me speak." Asking them all to be quiet, he spoke, addressing himself to the Chickasaws. He explained to them the nature and uses of the animal whose hide was before them; that it belonged to a great General, who lived on the other side of the Hatchie; that he strayed away from his shop into the thick cane last fall, while he was absent from home; that he and his neighbors had hunted for him for weeks, and concluded that he was caught in the overflow and drowned; that he had to pay the General six hundred dollars for his loss; that he was a poor man, not able to pay that big money; that he had been good to them, fixing and repairing their old guns whenever they came to him, and never charged them much; that the Chickasaws were a brave, honorable nation; that they had never stolen anybody's property, nor trespassed upon anyone's rights. The brave young man, who was the best shot and won the hide, acknowledged that he killed him. He was satisfied that he thought he was shooting some wild animal; that he felt innocent of doing harm. Yet, they were in the white man's country, where laws were made; that the laws did not have any respect to persons, and ignorance was no excuse; that all were alike guilty, and they must pay him for killing the animal. If they refused, the man of the law was upon the ground, who would have them all arrested and carried to jail.

The utmost respect and attention was paid to Barnes while he was making this plain talk. The older heads of the red men gathered together in the grove, and held council in the matter. After a long talk, the young hunters having gathered around them, they dispersed, each man going to his pony. Their movements were eagerly watched and noted by the thirty good marksmen at the shop. Getting their ponies, they all came leading them up before the shop. An intelligent looking old hunter spoke:

"We sorry for killing him. We think he belong to the woods. We find him in thick cane. We think him wild. We sorry for Barn—good man, work much. We take no white man's hoss, pony, nothin that b'longs to white man. We honest. We pay. We have ponies; that's all [motioning toward the long line of ponies held by their owners.] Take pay. We honest."

The strategy was a success. The red men had shown themselves true CHICKASAWS. Barnes told his red friends to point out the ponies they wanted to give up in payment for the jack. The old hunter who had acted as spokesman said: "Take, take plenty. Red man pay white man. Let white man say." Barnes then suggested that three white men and two red men be appointed as appraisers. They were appointed, and passed upon the value of the ponies, fixing their value at seventeen dollars and a fraction as the average, turning over to Barnes thirty-five ponies in payment and full satisfaction for his jack. What became of General Tipton's jackass was satisfactorily explained.

The Chickasaws meeted out a full measure of justice to our friend Barnes—six hundred dollars' worth of ponies satisfied the law. It was their first lesson—stunning lesson under the teachings of stern, written law. They would have no more of it, so they cut short their hunt, and bid a long farewell to the Big Hatchie country, their old hunting ground, and returned to their "beloved prairies," soon to be yielded up to the progress of Southern agriculture. Barnes had a public sale and sold off the ponies, distributing the *illegitimate* proceeds of his jack through the settlement, thereby increasing the stock of the land. My eldest brother purchased three of them; most excellent hunting ponies they were.

It is proper to mention here, that the parties at Bolivar, who became possessed of the jack's hide, and who enjoyed the joke, had it *narrated* in the lower settlement, where the Indians were wont to hunt, putting on foot inquiries as to who had lost a jack-ass, which came to the knowledge of the owners thereof. For none stood higher for commercial integrity than the merchants of Bolivar.

BOLIVAR

was one of the earliest and most important trading posts in West Tennessee. Its first settlers were men of a high grade—such men as the Polks, Bills, Woods, Millers, McNeils, and many others, whose names are not only identified with Bolivar and Hardeman county, but familiar to the whole Western District of Tennessee as among the best and brightest. Of the many old settlers, whose long and eventful life has been spared to link the past with the present, and who stands among the noble fathers of the land, no better specimen could be offered than the name of

PITSER MILLER.

I well remember him at the period, when my father, with his immigrant train, camped at Bolivar, waiting for the waters of the Big Hatchie to subside to enable him to cross. He was then quite a young man, of course. He came to our camp, made the acquaintance of my mother, and would have her and my grandmother, and the young children, to go to his house, and showed them every kindness—not letting them leave his hospitable roof until the train was ready to move across the river. His generous kindness was ever remembered by my father and mother, and will never be forgotten by their children. I am not aware, at this writing, whether he is among the living, but if gone forever, his name will long survive his mortal death. I regret that I am not able to give a biographical sketch of him—such as his name merits, as I knew him more from his high character than as a personal acquaintance. Certain it is, however, that the annals of West Tennessee could not be written without his name. He ever stood with the people of Bolivar and Hardeman county as the first and leading merchant, and exercised and maintained a healthy influence over all who knew him and enjoyed his acquaintance. I remember that one earnest sentence spoken by him, so influenced my mother as to have turned the scale of fortune against us. My father, upon reaching Bolivar, had not determined upon a point of location. He had several landed interests in Tennessee. He had visited the country the year previous, and explored it from the first to the fourth Chickasaw bluff. He had stood upon the grand bluff upon which the magnificent young city of Memphis now stands, when Bayou Gayoso coursed its way through a wild jungle—the haunts of the wild beast—and communed with the grand river He was interested with the late Colonel John C. Maclemore (who was a near relative of my mother), in several landed interests. Among the tracts in which he had an interest, was the Ramsay five-thousand-acre tract, now covered by South Memphis. It had been agreed between Colonel Maclemore and my father, that he could, at his option, locate upon the Ramsay tract. It was his aim and wish to settle upon the banks of the great river Mississippi, in hearing of its surging waters. The subject was being freely discussed in the presence of Mr. Miller. My mother had given the subject but little thought, so charmed was she with Pitser Miller. My father, however, had the fourth Chickasaw bluff firmly set in his heart. Mr. Miller remained reticent as to an opinion upon the subject until my mother, addressing him, called for his opinion. In all seriousness he said: "*Well Madam, if you will go and settle on the banks of the Mississippi river, let me suggest that your husband take along plank enough to make coffins to bury your children—your whole family.*" I remember well the electric effect of these remarks upon my mother. Her children were her jewels—eight of them. My father, be it said, ever yielded to the fancies of his intelligent and loving wife, Patsey. The decision was taken, and Pitser Miller's *coffin plank* kept us from settling on the Ramsay tract. Nobody is responsible for the freaks of Dame Fortune—an unmitigated old hag, unworthy of decent burial. Our immigrant train had better have turned in the direction of the fourth Chickasaw bluff, with Mr. Miller's coffin plank, than to have crossed the Big Hatchie. Yet, Dame Fortune never cast "new-comers" upon a more enchanting and lovely spot than fell to our lot north of the Big Hatchie. This incident is only mentioned to show the influence Pitser Miller exercised over the minds of men—especially *women*—even in his *young* days.

Returning to our wilderness home, our greatest need was good bread. The steel mill had worn out, and we had to resort to the mortar and pestle. The meanest of all meal is that pounded in a mortar—a wooden mortar—*dark, dingy, close, clammy.* Bread made of it is *too mean to write about.* So my father resolved to build a mill. Selecting for it a beautiful site on the creek, where the bluff was most inviting, he went to work with his own resources, and soon had an old time "tub-mill" ready to make good meal. He sent up in the vicinity of Jackson, in Madison county, for his mill-rocks. He also attached a gin, for we had began to grow cotton. He purchased his gin-stand of

JOSHUA FARRINGTON,

of Brownsville, than whom no cleverer man ever filed a saw-tooth or adjusted a brush. I remember Mr. Farrington as a true type of an old-time gentleman. His gins, manufactured by himself and sons, were, as to West Tennessee, what Pratt's were to Alabama. By his industry and probity he raised a large family of sons and daughters, who became ornaments in society—his eldest, Jacob, the popular, enterprising man of progress; John, eminent as a jurist, and William, prominent as a merchant and financier, and now stands head among the bank presidents of Memphis. John and William are, I believe, all that are now living of the worthy sons of a most worthy sire. The mill going, and gin ready, a press was needed, but where to get a screw-cutter was the trouble. My father, inquiring in the settlement, was informed that there was an excellent screw-cutter, who had abandoned his trade and taken to bear-hunting; that his place of dwelling, or camp, as it was termed, was somewhere over on Cane creek. He forthwith dispatched old Jack, with such instructions as he could give him. The next day, about noon, Jack returned, bringing the screw-cutter with him. He came on foot, with a heavy, short rifle on his shoulder, in well-dressed leather overalls up to his hips, followed by two ferocious dogs, of immense size, panther-colored, with black, broad noses, their ears rounded off close to their heads, and their tails bobbed off close to their broad haunches--brother and sister. They were the best-trained bear-dogs in the Big Hatchie country, and their owner the best hunter in Crockett's land. A model bear-hunter, he had hunted with David Crockett, and was familiar with the range and haunts of bruin from Reelfoot lake to the mouth of the Hatchie. Stout and strong (he stood full six feet), straight as an Iroquois, carrying no surplus flesh, with an iron constitution, his home and delight was the wildwoods; intelligent and good looking, withal, and as unselfish as the genial soil upon which he was wont to tread. Preferring the chase to work, the utilitarian would write him down as a lazy man. He soon satisfied my father that he could cut a screw—that he was a finished workman—but he was loth to take the job, as it was near the hunting season (it was then early fall), and he could not come and leave his family in his camp, as he called it. He had a wife and two young children, twin daughters, and not a year old. My mother, overhearing the conversation, and equally anxious about the screw, spoke, saying: "Oh, no, sir! It will never do to leave your wife and her babies alone in the woods. Bring them along; we will provide for them some way. We can fix them up in the loom-house; it has a good fire-place, and we will not need it until the cotton is picked out and ginned. Beside, if you want to hunt bear, you can find as many down the creek as on Reelfoot lake." The question of the screw-cutter coming was soon settled, and it was agreed that Jack should hitch up a team and return with him that evening, and move his family over immediately. The screw-cutter remarked that two horses and a light wagon would be sufficient, as his wife constituted the heaviest part of his household goods. It was so. Old Jack returned in the afternoon of the next day, bringing the screw-cutter and all of his earthly possessions, consisting of wife and two babies, and but little else besides the scanty bed upon which they slept, and they were as happy as if they had rosewood and mahogany, damask and satin. Young and healthy, they lived in and for one another. Without doubt my recollection pictures her the handsomest looking woman, for her flesh and size, I ever saw—tall, above the average height of woman, and remarkably well-shaped and fleshy. Two hundred pounds was her ordinary weight. Her features were faultless, and her complexion as delicate as a rose-leaf. Her two babies were as fat and beautiful as herself. My mother thought her a sweet woman, and became quite fond of her. She, like her husband, was intelligent and interesting in conversation, and, like him, the wild-woods was her delight. The screw-cutter pushed his screw-cutting work on rapidly, so as to get into the woods. He proved to be an excellent workman, and my father built him a house near the mill, where he lived several years, rendering himself serviceable when called upon. During the bear-hunting season he was for the most part in the woods with his rifle and two dogs. His house was never clear of bear-bacon. The screw and press being finished, the mill and gin going, an appointment was made for a big bear-hunt, to begin at the Big Hurricane, some eight miles up the river, and hunt down. The coming among us of the model bear-hunter, with his two well-trained dogs, Cæsar and Bess, excited the amateur hunters of the settlement to go into a hunt with him, and see his famous dogs handle a bear. The time fixed to go into the hunt was to be a week before Christmas, and to end New-Year's day.

There were but few expert bear-hunters in the settlement. Among them, and perhaps the best, was Cary Estes. His elder brother, Captain Albert, was an expert hunter also, but had not the passion for it that Cary had. Both of them had a pack of well-trained bear-dogs. Pendleton Gaines, familiarly known as "Pet," was a good hunter; so was his brother Ab, but he was fat, and fond of his ease, and couldn't *last* on a *big run.* Steptoe Johnson was always ready to go into a hunt, but was never up to the "*killing.*" I had grown large and strong enough to shoot "off-hand" with a rifle, and had killed my bear, a four-hundred-and-sixty-pound one, at that, when lean in flesh, and had succeeded to the "little rifle."

I may be pardoned for giving a brief account of my "first killing," before going into the big hunt. It was a part of my assigned duty to drive the cows up every evening. Sometimes I rode—oftener I did not, and when going on foot, my next younger brother went with me. I mentioned that I had succeeded to the "little rifle," and she was ever on my shoulder when in the woods. I had a little Scotch bull terrier—Tasso. Tasso was my constant companion during daylight; he went with me, of course. We set off early in the afternoon, on one of the last days in August. The cows were in the habit of feeding a mile or more away from the house. Their favorite grazing was on the walnut level, a level bench of land on the Hatchie Bottom, where the wild pea most abounded. It was free from undergrowth, and thickly studded with walnut, hickory and ash. This lovely bench of land bordered on the Big Slough, where commenced an almost impenetrable canebrake, extending into the river, some half mile off. We found the cows where expected. A familiar whoop started them homeward, the old "bell cow" taking the lead. The sun was then an hour high, and we stalked around on the Big Slough for a little hunt. We had gone but a short distance when, passing around the lap of a large fallen tree, a yearling deer sprang out, scampered off some forty yards, and stopped by a large clay-root. The barrel of the "little rifle" was ready and leveled upon the little fellow in an instant. Upon his bringing a halt, the sharp crack of the rifle startled the hooting owl, and with it came the shrill, distressing bleat of the fawn. I had shot too far back, breaking him down in the loins. Its bleating was most distressing. I had heard old hunters say that wild beasts of prey would come to the bleating of a fawn as far as they could hear it. Our proximity to the known haunts of the bear and the panther instantly aroused my fears, and I fell to reloading my rifle. I had not more than got the charge of powder to the muzzle, when a startling crash and cracking of the cane was heard across the slough. Before I had time to patch my bullet, we heard a plunge into the water, and the next moment a monster bear came up the bank of the slough, making his way to where the fawn was bleating. Tasso had by this time slipped from us, and reached the fawn simultaneously with the bear, disputing his right to interfere. In the mean time the fawn had worked his way behind the clay-root, from where we were standing, and out of our view. Tasso and the monster were engaging one another over the little deer, which continued its bleating. Soon we heard the brave little dog squall out, as though he had received a death-blow. He ceased barking, and my fears were that it was "up with him." I ran down a naked bullet, and went on the double-quick, under cover of the large clay-root, to my little dog's relief. Reaching the spot I mounted the log, which brought my head and shoulders above the clay-root. The fawn had crawled some distance from the two contending hosts. Tasso was in the folds of the bear's huge arms, grappling with all his might under the throat of the monster, which was doing his best to hug—to squeeze the little fellow to death. His size alone saved him from having every bone in his little body crushed. Fretted so by Tasso, he had not discovered me, then within ten feet of him. I surveyed the situation, so as not to endanger my little dog's life by an unlucky shot, not being able, from his position, and the constant motion of his head, to put a bullet in the burr of his ear. Old bruin sat square upon his broad haunches, with his back to me. I aimed well, and put a ball through his loins, over the region of the kidneys, sprawling the monster his full length upon the ground, and Tasso was saved. Reloading, I sent a bullet through his brain, ending his misery. I had expected to find my little dog badly hurt, and was greatly delighted to find that he was only bitten through the ball of one of his fore feet, carrying away a couple of his toes. My brother, who had been a quiet looker-on, had taken charge of the little deer, which kept up its bleating until relieved by the hunting-knife.

The sun had gone down—it was growing dark in the bottom, and we were a mile and a half away from home. The fawn we could have carried, but there lay stretched out a monster bear, which, had it been fat, would have weighed six or more hundred pounds. It was my first bear, too. I felt that I could build up a fire and spend the night with him—would have done so, rather than leave him, so proud was I of my "*first killing.*" I commenced blowing my horn—(every one, in those days, who went into the woods, carried a blowing horn, and none could blow a horn better than "we boys"). I continued to blow it at intervals, knowing it would soon be answered by the big horn from home. In the mean time we struck fire. To strike fire, in the days of flint locks, was an easy matter. Sharpen a stick, force it tight into the touch-hole, fill the pan with powder, and you could strike fire without endangering the "going-off" of your gun. We put fire to the tree-cap, and the leaves, being dry, and still clinging to the limbs, the lurid flames went high in the tree-tops, lighting up the woods for a hundred or more yards around. Blowing again, we were answered by the big horn. My father, followed by old Jack, soon rode up, inquiring what was the matter. Pointing to my first "killing," the matter fully explained itself. The bright light from the tree-top exposed to view the black monster and the innocent little deer, with its spots not yet passed off. The matter of the killing being explained to my father, he turned to Jack and gave him the order to return home in haste and tell Jim to hitch one yoke of his oxen to the fore-wheels of the wagon which he had been using during the day in hauling house-logs, and come with quick haste down the river road to a certain big log, and turn into the walnut level, bringing several of the men with him. Within a short hour Jim, with Bright and Darling yoked to the fore-wheels of the wagon, was making his way through the open woods to where we were. In another hour we were at home with my first "killing," and I was the recipient of all sorts of flattering remarks and comments from mother, brothers, and all the darkies. From that day I was numbered among the bear-hunters. I had often been along with the hunters—followed up the chase and witnessed the killing, but this was *my first killing.* The circumstances of the killing were recounted to the screw-cutter. His comments and remarks as to my manner and coolness displayed, filled me almost to bursting with self-importance, and I became his favorite hunting companion. I remember well that wakeful night. My young thoughts lingered and hovered around that clay-root all night. The pitiful bleating of the fawn; the startling crash and cracking of the cane, as the monster bear came rushing through it; the piercing squall of my little Tasso; the great bear sitting upon his broad haunches, with the brave little dog in the folds of his huge arms, and the little fellow grappling him under his throat, were scenes fresh with me all night, whether awake or dreaming.

Pardon me, reader, for keeping you out of the big hunt so long. We will go into it in the next chapter.

CHAPTER V.

Big Bear-Hunt—Temple, the Model Bear-Hunter, and His Dogs Cæsar and Bess—The Big Hurricane—Numerous Bear Killings—Encounter with a Panther—Roosting Wild Turkeys—Camp Life in the Woods—The Locked Buck Horns—The Deer Lick Slosh—The Big Bear—The Killing—Camp Stories and Anecdotes—The Last Day's Hunt and the Last Killing.

Now, reader, we are ready for the big bear-hunt. Already a month has elapsed since it was talked about. Temple was loth to go into it. An old and experienced hunter, owning two of the best trained and most valuable dogs in the Big Hatchie country, and fearing, from the inexperienced and often reckless shooting, that they would as likely be the victims of the shots as the bear, it was not surprising that he should feel a reluctance in joining in the hunt. He promised to go in, however, and was true to his word; beside, he was curious to know something of the Big Hurricane. Tuesday before Christmas was the day appointed to meet; the place of rendezvous, at a point named near the Big Hurricane, ten or more miles up the river. It was understood that every hunter take with him a man-servant, except Temple. My father declined going, but promised to join in if the hunt should extend down in his hunting-ground. Steptoe would'nt go unless my father went; beside, he was getting old, and his old gray mare was lean in flesh. The signs, as to the weather, were favorable. We had had a dry winter up to that time, and the bottom was right for a good run.

Temple and myself set off, as soon as we could see, to follow a blind trail leading up the bottom, followed by old Jack. Our course led through good hunting woods. I suggested to Temple that he had better "yoke his dogs; they might strike a fresh scent, which might delay our reaching the ground at the appointed time." "Oh, no, they wait for the word to 'go in.' I shall certainly not give it to them." Jogging along single file, at a six-mile pace, we soon reached Big Creek. Finding an easy ford, we crossed without difficulty, hurrying on to the Big Lagoon, where we encountered difficulty in finding a crossing. It is an ugly, muddy stream, with a miry bottom. Turning up it, we came to a shallow ford. The opposite bank presented a high bluff; we crossed, however, riding near the water's edge until reaching an abrupt bend, where the bluff terminated. The banks of the lagoon, from which we crossed, was thickly studded with tall cane, the tops bending down to the water's edge. Coming to the abrupt bend, Temple, who was riding before, reined up his horse, and pointing up the lagoon, remarked, in a low tone of voice: "What a pity! what a pity! Old fellow, we must hands off; it will never do to draw blood before we get together and organize." The object of his remarks was a huge bear, in the act of lapping water, standing on the margin of the stream, on the opposite bank, broadside toward us, and within easy rifle range. He raised his great head, and deliberately viewed us, seemingly unconcerned—a most tempting shot. Cæsar and Bess were not slow in discovering him. With a fixed gaze, the hair down their backs standing at an angle of forty-five degrees, they looked up at their master now and then for the word to "go in." I begged for a shot. Temple replied: "No; it will not do; it is a pity to pass him, but it must be so. We will get him this evening or to-morrow. He is housed up not an hundred yards from where he is taking water. Lets go." Turning to the right, up the bank, we went on our way in the direction of the Big Hurricane, then two or more miles away. Reaching the vicinity of the place where we were to meet, Temple blew his horn; it was answered, and we soon joined Cary and Captain Albert. Pet and Ab had not yet arrived. They were soon up, and all dismounted for a talk. Six hunters were present, including my little self. The Captain and Cary were comparative strangers to Temple. Cary was regarded as the most experienced and expert hunter present, and specially familiar with the Big Hurricane and its surroundings. Earnest in speech, more truthful and reliable than is common to hunters, he was expected to open the subject of organizing the hunt. Addressing himself to Temple, he said:

"Well, Mr. Temple, we have appointed this hunt that we might have the pleasure of having you with us, and to see your celebrated dogs handle a bear.

Your celebrity as a bear-hunter is known to us. We have come prepared for several days' hunt, if it should prove agreeable. Though a young man, and a comparative young hunter, I have found, by experience, that to hunt bear properly and successfully, where there is more than one hunter in the hunt, it is best that we be perfectly agreed as to the order and rules that should govern us. I propose, therefore, Mr. Temple, that you suggest the rules that shall govern us in the hunt." Temple spoke slowly and distinctly, approving heartily what had been said, remarking further, that it had been his misfortune to have drawn out of hunts for the lack of order and a good understanding. "I make it a rule for instance, that when a 'start' is made, if any of the hunters should halloo out to encourage the dogs, I call mine off and quit. It is also a rule with me, that if any of the hunters should, by accident or reckless shooting, wound or kill a dog, I draw out and take my dogs, or he is required to do so. I have noticed that the over anxious, hasty hunter, is more apt to scare the bear than kill him, and as often shoots a dog, when in a close fight, as the bear. My dogs are trained to stay with me until I give them the word to go. They fight close—too close sometimes—when the bear is wounded. When hunting alone, I never have to shoot the second time. I have trained them to hold a bear at bay, at the risk of getting scratched. When I think he aims to make a big run, I let the slut go in; otherwise I keep her with me. The dog is usually enough to hold any bear in check until I get up. Neither of then give 'mouth,' when on a 'run.' When 'up,' they take him above the elbow of the fore-arm, until they bring him to a 'stop,' then they bark a few minutes, and wait for my coming. If I am not up soon, they give 'mouth' again. The few rules which are known to all good bear-hunters being observed, we will have a pleasant and agreeable hunt. I should have mentioned that no dog should be allowed in the hunt that will run a deer or anything else but a bear or panther."

Temple's suggestions were heartily agreed to, and the hunt was organized, Cary being chosen leader. Captain Albert and Ab, with three of the negroes, went to select a suitable place to camp, on a small branch running into the lagoon, a short distance below. Cary, Pet, Temple and myself filed off for a short hunt. Temple had related the circumstance of our having seen the bear in crossing the lagoon. It was agreed that we go and take him, remarking that he knew pretty much his run. We were soon on the bluff overlooking the dense cane-brake in which he was "housed." Cary suggested that he knew a good crossing a half mile above; that he and Pet would go up and cross, and come down the lagoon, outside of the thick cane, which would insure his taking down the stream, or crossing it, about where we saw him taking water; that we remain on the bluff until the "start," when we could determine his movements. "You can put your dogs in, Mr. Temple, when you think it best." Cary and Pet rode away. Temple and myself remained on the high bluff. Seating ourselves upon a large log, we quietly interested ourselves noticing the movements of Cæsar and Bess. They took their stand on the brink of the bluff, gazing across the lagoon in the supposed direction where the bear was "housed," throwing their heads one side now and then, to catch the first sound that should come across from the hunters or dogs. Temple, pointing to an opening in the dense forest that overshadowed the cane-brake, remarked:

"I'll bet Cæsar's ears that he is 'housed up' among the old logs in that opening, where the cane is thickest."

He had hardly finished speaking, when the dogs broke out in a fierce bay at the very place.

"There he is now; hold! The whole pack is upon him."

Cæsar and Bess stood trembling, looking around every moment for their master to say "go."

"Bless me!" says Temple, "what mouths! That fuss ought to start the devil himself from his den. Hark! we will soon hear a shot! Notice the lull in the dog's baying. The hunters are close up."

In a moment the sharp crack of the rifle rang through the woods, followed by the crash of the cane.

"Bad shot. He is out, now, for a big run. The dogs can't hold him in that thick cane. He aims to go down. Let's be off."

Down under the bluff we went, crossing at the same place where we had crossed in the morning. Ascending the opposite bank, we immediately passed into an open glade, running out for a hundred or more yards. The bear and dogs, judging from their course as indicated by the sounds, would pass through the glade. The dogs were making a desperate effort to hold him in the cane. Just then a yearling bear came dashing out of the cane from the direction of the dogs, entering the glade near us.

"Don't shoot!" said Temple.

He gave the word to Cæsar and Bess to "Take!" In less than sixty yard's run they overhauled him. When we got up, they had him snatched. Temple drew out his long knife and dispatched him. By this time the big bear entered the glade, passing within forty yards of us. The pack were up with him. As he cleared the cane he made an opening of several yards between himself and the hounds, when Cæsar and Bess were told to "go in." Making their best run, they brought him to a "stop" as he was about entering the cane on the opposite side of the glade.

"Take your time, hunters, he will go no further," said Temple, as we joined Cary and Pet, in pursuit, on a big run.

They brought a halt, and we closed in upon the exciting scene, taking our time. Reaching within safe shooting distance, Cary said to Temple, "Give him the first shot."

"No," says Temple; "let him who shot first try it again."

The bear was making a desperate effort to get away, the dogs fighting him close. Cæsar and Bess were dividing their strength on either side of him, both fast hold of his arms above the hock or elbow, bringing him now and then upon his knees, and the half-hounds pinching him close in behind. Bear was never worried more. Pet stood with his rifle leveled. It being his second shot, he wanted it to be a death-shot. Temple's dogs completely covered his sides with their bodies; his head was in constant motion, swinging and snapping, first one side and then the other, and it was next to impossible to put his bullet in his brain. Pet, already worried from intense excitement, approached nearer, but was still unable to find a safe place to put his bullet with telling effect. In the meantime, the dogs pressed the old fellow so hard, in his madness he rose upon his hind legs, and, making a desperate effort to rid himself of the dogs, made a surprising leap, reaching a tree standing near, carrying Bess up with him. Temple's quick eye discovered her peril, and sent a well-aimed ball under the burr of the monster's ear before he had got more than fifteen feet from the ground, his slut still holding her grip. The bear fell, falling upon her. Temple was soon to her relief, rolling the monster off of her. She was none the worse off, however, for her fall. The dogs gathered around him, pinching him, now and then, to see if he was dead. The hunters stood around in gleeful delight, remarking upon the fight and the dexterous skill of Cæsar and Bess in handling a bear.

"It surpasses anything I have ever witnessed in all my bear-hunting career. Your dogs, Mr. Temple, surpass even what I had expected of them. Were they mine, I would value them above the price of a small plantation."

"Yes," said Temple, "they have behaved very well in this fight. I was fearful that Bess would be hard to satisfy. I seldom let her go in upon a wounded bear. Beside, she and the dog had just drawn their teeth out of a yearling bear when I let them in this fight."

"A yearling bear!" said Cary; "when, and where?"

"Less than two hundred yards out yonder in the slash you will find a yearling bear stretched out on the ground. As we crossed the lagoon and entered the opening the little fellow came dashing out of the cane, scared up by yonder dogs. I told my dogs to 'take,' and in a few jumps they overhauled him. When we got up they had the little fellow stretched out on the ground. I knifed him, leaving him as he lay, and told the dogs to go in this fight, and joined you and friend Pet, as we did."

Turning to me he asked if I would go with the boys (a couple of them had just come up) and have him dragged up, and we would butcher them both on the same ground. The yearling was soon laying beside the monster.

I will mention here that a bear less than a year old is called a "cub." The cubs gang with their dam until they are a year old; they then take to themselves, and are called yearlings until they are two years old. Parturition with the bear generally takes place in February. The yearling knifed by Temple was about twenty-one months old. Pet was examining the bear for signs of his bullet-hole.

"You must have missed him," said Cary.

"Well, I reckon I did, as I can't find any bullet-hole except the one in his head. The cane was very thick between him and me when I fired. My ball must have struck one and turned."

"Well, we had as well commence taking off the old fellow's hide," says Cary. "Come, boys, out with your knives."

Taking hold of one of his great paws, he remarked:

"Old fel, you have made your last run. I have had this old bear on a good many runs, Mr. Temple; he is an old acquaintance in these woods. Had he have gotten to the Big Hurricane, where he was aiming to go, it would have been a sore thing to have gotten him out. We may thank your dogs for his hide *this time.*"

His hide was soon off. Pet examined again, but couldn't find his bullet-hole. Quartered and packed, Cary took from behind his saddle a cord carried for such purposes, cut a slit through the under jaw of the yearling into his mouth, noosed the cord around his neck, passing the end through the slit into his mouth, and made it fast to his horse's tail. Spreading the little fellow upon his belly, it was announced that we were ready for the camp. Starting off down the lagoon, remarking that we would find an easy crossing below, we all followed, with prospects of a tender bear-steak for supper. It was surprising to see with what ease the little bear was cordelled over logs and rough places. Remarking upon it, Cary said it was the way he took most of his bear home; that he "had frequently carried a three-hundred-and-fifty-pound bear six or eight miles home, tied to his horse's tail."

We soon reached the camp, admirably located for a sort of winter quarters. The boys had a blazing, hot hickory fire ready for us. Night was hedging in fast, and Pete, the leading butcher (the Captain's servant), was told to hurry up; that steaks were wanted from the yearling for supper. Ab was a sort of head steward in camp. His looks and proportions had marked him out for one—fat, and fond of good eating himself. Only too fond of good whisky—any kind of whisky—he groaned heavily when the article was ruled out of camp. The yearling's steaks were ready for the pan, tender as a kid, and his fat ribs just right for roasting. Bread, potatoes and salt were all that was brought into camp. For meat we depended upon the woods. The Captain was not in camp. Inquiry was made after him. Pete said that he had gone to "roost" a gang of wild turkies, and would be back soon.

Cary remarked: "Yes; I have known him to spend night after night after turkies. Getting into a gang, he would keep on shooting until he had the last one of them."

Just then the Captain came in, very quiet in his movement. He carefully put away his gun. It was cold, and he looked it. Squaring himself down upon a bear-skin, all waited for him to give an account of his movements, or for some one to question him as to what he had done. He finally broke the silence.

"Well, I see you have brought in plenty of meat. Good luck for a short hunt."

"Yes," said Cary, "we not only had luck, but more fun and excitement than is usual in a short hunt," then recounting the full particulars, as they occurred.

"I was satisfied, when I saw Mr. Temple's dogs, that they were all right. I hope to have the pleasure of seeing them in a fight to-morrow. Seeing a large gang of turkies make off toward the bottom, as we were fixing to pitch camp here, I concluded that I would go and roost them. Large gang of fat gobblers! Pete, we will go after them as soon as the moon gets above the trees." (The moon was then in her second quarter, and had risen.)

"Yes, sir, Pete will be with Mars Albert when he goes! Now, come and eat, Mars Albert. They have all eaten, and here is a panfull of nice, tender bear-steak. Come while it's hot."

The Captain responded to Pete's invitation. The moon being in the right position for the Captain to "go for" his turkies, started, followed by Pete. No one was invited to go with him. He had been gone but a short while when we heard him shoot. Soon he shot again, and again, until we counted seven shots within a short hour. By eleven he and Pete were back, loaded. Pete had four, and the Captain two. Throwing down his six fat gobblers, the Captain remarked that he had killed the seventh, but that it fell across the lagoon.

"Pete," says he, "you must go after that turkey in the morning; do you hear?"

"Yes, *Mars Albert.* Pete hears, and he gwine after him in the morning, be sure that I will."

Adjusting ourselves around the fire, with our heads pillowed on saddles, we slept till early morning. Our first morning in the woods, we were up before day, talking over the hunt before us. We were to hunt the Big Hurricane. Guns had been shot off, wiped out, reloaded and freshly primed. The gray streaks of the early morn indicated a sunshiny day. The sun was not yet up, and we had not eaten breakfast. The ribs were roasting and the steaks frying. While waiting, Temple remarked to Cary that he would like to know something more of the Big Hurricane—enough to enable him to get out of it if he should get in.

"Well," said Cary, "it is a mile or so above us, on the river. The river touches it, or it touches the river, in two places, about a quarter of a mile from where we will strike it, and again at its extreme upper end. It is about a mile and a half—perhaps more—long, and about one-third as wide. The river leaves it where it first strikes it as we go up, making a big bend. This bend takes in, perhaps, as much as three hundred acres—is, for the most part, overflowed land, mostly open; fine hunting woods. Where the bend elbows it is high, dry land, and is formed into an island by the river making a cut-off in high water. This island is a thick canebrake. The Hurricane will best describe itself when you see it and go into it. I will say, however, that there is not an original tree in it. All were blown down or topped off by the tornado that passed over it; when, no one knows. From the appearance of the undergrowth, it must have been ages ago. Near the river it is thick cane; the middle and outer portion, every variety of scrubby undergrowth, filled up with briers. Except for the rotting out of the old fallen trees, or logs—many, however, are yet in a sound state of preservation—egress into, or out of it, would be impossible. The wild beasts and *varmints* that have made it their haunts and homes for ages, have made many of these narrow openings smooth and hard by their frequent travels. It is just the thickest thicket you were ever in, Mr. Temple; but you will know more of it, before evening. Pete has announced breakfast. Let's eat and be off."

"Well," said Temple, "I feel that I have already been in it, from your description. It's no place to hunt bear. But to gratify a curiosity I have, I would, as a bear-hunter, turn my face from it."

"And so would I. As a hunter, I fully agree with you. I have lost more time, and had more dogs killed, and lost more game in it, than anywhere else. My object in wishing you to join us up here was to take, if possible, an old bear that has worried us and our dogs for more than three seasons, and carries in his huge body more than a half dozen bullets out of my rifle. We have followed him on a run from the Hurricane to the mouth of Cane creek, more than fifteen miles, and back, in the same day, losing him in the Hurricane. He is a monster, and it is worth a week's hunt to take him."

"Well, we will try, to-day."

"Come," sadi Cary, "let's go."

We were all off for the Big Hurricane, on foot, of course. A short half hour brought us to the high bluff where the Hurricane reaches the river. It became so thick and impenetrable that we were forced to wind our way down to the water's edge and clamber under the bluff until we reached the bend in the river where it leaves the Hurricane. We had not more than gotten in the open bottom when the dogs gave evidence that a bear or a panther was about. "Old Start" raised his smellers, and with stiffening tail he went off up the river in the bend, followed by the other half-hounds. They were soon on a running trail. Our sprightly young leader seemed impressed with the same spirit that animated the dogs. Hastily telling Temple to follow him, and the rest to string out along the Hurricane, he was off, following the dogs. We strung out as directed. The Captain, being a quick and fast runner, he was off. I kept close up with him, Pet and Ab behind. We could hear the increased cry of the dogs as we ran. Making a couple of hundred yards or more, the Captain halted, to get a better ear of the movements of the dogs, when we discovered that they were on a full run, in full cry, coming in the direction of the Hurricane, aiming to pass in above us. We moved up a little and waited. The Captain remarked that we would hardly reach the jungle before the dogs would bring the animal to a stop. "Bless me, what music." Fourteen dogs in full cry, soon in the morning, clear as a bell, not a breeze to disturb sound, in the open wood, and the pack in full, excited cry, was music most ravishing to the hunter's ear. On they come! Now we see him! He is a monster of his kind, black, burly, and ferocious-looking, running straight as an arrow toward us. Now the dogs gain on him—he is making his best run—running for dear life. Cæsar leads—leaves the pack, and is fast gaining on him, giving no mouth. He runs straight and swift, as if accelerated by electric force! He is upon him! The yellow is in contrast with the black! He takes him by the fore-arm! His run is broken! He stops him, and the pack is upon him! Bless me, how intensely exciting! Let's go up and enjoy the fight! The Captain and myself moved up. The scene was so exciting that we were in no hurry to dispatch him. Approaching nearer, the bear discovered us, and made a desperate plunge to get away. He had made but few bounds before Cæsar brought him to a stop again, when the half-hounds fought more vigorously, pinching him wherever they could get a hold. The bear was getting desperate, and the fight hot—"too hot," said the Captain. "Some of the dogs will get hurt. Shoot him!"

I replied that it was a dangerous place to shoot into; that he was more experienced, and for him to shoot, and shoot quick. He still insisted that I shoot first. Not hesitating again, for I had become all anxious to shoot, I approached within ten feet and watched my opportunity for the dogs to make an opening. It soon offered, and I fired, putting my ball in the region of his heart. In an instant he swung his great head around, biting at the place where the bullet had stung him, when the Captain fired, lodging a ball in his brain, abruptly terminating one of the most interesting and exciting bear-fights it was ever hunter's lot to witness. The hunters were all up at the killing. Temple remarked that the Captain and myself had had sport enough for one day.

"Yes," said Cary, "but we have something on hand likely to be a little more exciting. Mr. Temple and I have agreed to have a little ugly fun after a panther. We can take him in less than thirty minutes, unless he has already hurried himself into the Hurricane. We saw his tracks as we were crossing a wet slash, a couple of hundred yards back. He had just passed. Bess was anxious to "go for" him. Just then Pete, Joe and Jack came in on a lope. They had been instructed to pass up on the outer side of the Hurricane, come around through the passable wood, and join us in the bottom. They had heard the dogs and our firing, which hurried them on. Leaving the dead bear in their charge, we went for the panther. Cary gave instructions that the hunters, excepting Temple, should hold a position between the dogs and the hurricane. He and Templeton moved off to where they had seen the fresh sign. Reaching the place, the half-hounds went off on a running trail up the river, which put the Captain, Pet, Ab and myself on a run to keep between them and the Hurricane. The Captain ahead, running perhaps a quarter, the dogs were discovered to be going from us in the direction of an island in the elbow, made by the cut-off. The Captain suggested that we pursue them. In a big run we went until reaching the cut-off, where we halted to learn the situation. Cary and Temple had just crossed the cut-off (it was then dry) and were entering the thick cane in the direction of the dogs. They had treed him, and the Captain's quick eye was not long in discovering him. He said to us standing near:

"See that fallen tree lodged in the fork of that big white oak; look in the fork and you will see him crouched upon the fallen tree, with his head toward the root."

"Yes, we see him! we see him!" we exclaimed.

The Captain was making ready to shoot, when Ab said:

"But, Cap., he is in an ugly fix there for a good shot, and he is more than a hundred yards off—a long shot."

"Yes; but if we go further we can't see him for the cane. See him drawing himself up, making ready to spring; he sees the hunters and is either aiming to spring upon one of them or leave," said the Captain, leveling his rifle upon him.

With a steady and unerring aim he fired. The panther made a marvelous leap in the direction of the root of the fallen tree. Not a sound except the sharp ring of the rifle and the echo disturbed the stillness for more than a minute, when a dog squalled, then another, and another, and then the dull report of a rifle. The panther had discovered Temple and Cary as they reached the opening in the cane made by a fallen tree, but the thick cane overhead prevented them from seeing him. The Captain's quick eye in seeing him making ready for the spring, and instant shot, was most opportune. The panther fell short of his aim and the dogs covered him; rising he dealt death and pain with his great paws, killing one dog outright and wounded two others severely. The thick cane and the sharp fight with the dogs prevented Temple and Cary from shooting. Making havoc among the dogs, he got hold of Bess; she was grappling under his broad throat, when Temple went to her relief with his knife. Letting Bess go, the monster furiously attacked Temple. Fearfully grappling him, with one of his heavy paws fast upon his left shoulder, the other around his body pinning his right fast, he was making a furious effort to stretch his broad jaws across his right shoulder close up to his neck. Temple, staggering back under the weight and desperate attack of the infuriated panther, was in a perilous situation. Cary, quickly as possible, was to his relief. Putting the muzzle of his rifle against the body of the panther over the region of the heart he fired, killing him instantly. In the mean time Temple had extricated his right arm from the folds of the panther, and, simultaneously with Cary's shot, sent his knife up to the hilt into his vitals.

Cary went to work examining Temple, thinking it miraculous if he was not seriously hurt. Finding blood upon his shoulder and on his shirt collar, he was insisting upon his stripping off for a better examination, when the Captain, the Gaines and myself came up. Temple was protesting against being hurt at all—only scratched a little. His leather blouse, lined with dressed buckskin, with other leather strappings, had protected him from the long claws of the panther.

The Captain, stooping down examining for his bullet-hole, remarked that he had only broken his lower jaw; that the distance he had shot was greater than he had expected, as his ball had fallen three inches. His aim was to lodge his bullet in his brain, but it fell below its aim. This discovery fully explained why Temple's shoulder and neck was not crushed and mangled by the monster's jaws, and accounted for his being stained with blood.

"Well, Mr. Leader," said Ab, addressing himself to Cary, "I guess you are satisfied now with what you call 'a little ugly fun.' Our friend has made a miraculous escape."

"Yes," said Cary, "we are satisfied. We knew it was a little out of our line, but it was tempting, and we came near paying well for it."

"What will we do with him?" asked the Captain. "Blow for the boys, or drag him to where they are?"

"Just as you all may say," said Cary.

"Drag him, of course," remarked Ab, and suiting his action to his words, he soon had a vine ready and noosed around his neck, and we moved to where Pete and his companions were butchering the bear.

"Pete," said the Captain, "skin him carefully; it's my hide" (the first blood always took the hide).

Leaving Pete and his companions butchering the bear and skinning the panther, the hunters moved off to hunt the Big Hurricane. It was then in the early forenoon, the right time of the day to go in. Reaching a deep wash, where it debouched into the open bottom, Cary brought a halt, and said:

"Now, Mr. Temple, here is what I call the mouth

of the 'Clay Gut;' it heads up in and drains a wet slash in the heart of the Hurricane. It is dry now, and we can walk up it. I call it the 'Clay Gut,' because it is washed out to the clay. It has, as you see, a hard clay bottom."

The hunters started up it, single file, to hunt for the oldest bear inhabitant of the woods. It had washed out six or eight feet deep. Winding up through the jungle, egress to or from it could only be made through the narrow openings made by the rotting out of the old logs; the trails were arched over by cane and vines; frequently small runs came into it, and we saw not the sun until we reached the slash.

Reaching the slash we halted to rest, when Cary remarked that he had been there only once. "It was," said he, "last November a year ago. Upon reaching the spot where we now are, I saw two large bucks with their horns locked; they seemed to be exhausted; and one was upon his knees. I shot the one standing, and killed the other with my knife. As I shot I saw a large panther move slowly away from near where they were standing, the same, most likely, we killed this morning; he was doubtless waiting to make his supper out of one of them, as he did, for I left them, not being able to take them away. They may have been locked together a day or more, judging from the manner in which the ground was torn up. They were the largest bucks I ever saw; you will say they are the largest deer horns you ever saw. I defy any one to pull them apart without breaking off a peg. We will go and find them; the panther certainly did not eat up the horns."

We went in search of the horns, but, reaching the spot where they were expected to be found, they were not there. Cary looked a little confounded, so certain was he of finding them where stated.

"Certainly no one has been here and taken them away. I have not been relating a dream," said he, looking again from the position where he stood when relating the story of the bucks. "Yes; it was here I left them. Let me take a look in the direction I saw the panther move away." Walking some sixty or more yards, he came to the edge of the cane. "Here they are," says he.

We all had become anxious to see the locked horns, and were soon with him. They had been dragged to the edge of the cane, and were still locked. It must have been a powerful beast to have done it. They were there and not yet separated from the head. Larger deer horns none professed ever to have seen. All hands took a pull and tried to separate them, but gave it up that it could not be done without "breaking a peg."

While we were discussing the horns, the dogs were exploring the surroundings. Numerous winding trails came into the slash from the jungle, smooth and hard—too hard to discover the foot-prints of the many travelers that passed over them. The opening made by the slash contained, perhaps, three acres, upon which no vegetation grew—it was a deer-lick.

"Hark!" said Cary, "that's old Start."

In a moment several of the half-hounds broke out

in a fierce bay. Moving across the slash, we had not reached the edge of the cane before the whole pack were in, barking furiously. Cæsar and Bess stood by their master waiting for the words "go in." The dogs were baying less than an hundred yards from where we stood, and it was impossible for man to get to them except upon his knees.

"Now," said the Captain, "if it should happen to be the oldest inhabitant, he will not leave if he is well housed; no, not so long as he can keep his tail-end protected. Some of us must slip in—crawl in —and give him a start."

"If crawling is to be done, my young hunter friend here," pointing to myself, "may be relied upon," said Temple.

"It is an ugly job for a grown man, but for a boy who has not forgotten how to crawl, he would be in his element," was my remark, accepting the honor.

I simply asked Temple to let his dogs "go in," and was off, examining my priming as I went. I soon found a winding trail in the right direction. Half bent I went in with heart palpitating—right up in my throat. Reaching within twenty yards, I came within full view of him and the dogs through a narrow vista, which was made by the rotting out of a large fallen tree, the stump of which formed the rear of his lair. The cane tops and vines had completely arched over the stump. With his back to the old stump, he was striking right and left at the approach of the dogs. Alive to the situation, knowing that I filled the only passway out, and that my shot must be a death one or be run over and possibly hurt by him, I resolved to wait my chance for a better shot. The dogs formed a half circle in front of him; his head was in perpetual motion. I waited for him to rise upon his hind feet, when I felt sure of putting my bullet in his heart. Suddenly Cæsar and Bess passed me, jumping over my left shoulder. The bear's attention was attracted by them, when he discovered me. Instantly he made a leap, leaping clear of the dogs in front. I had gotten over the bear-buck-ague, and felt steady. My rifle was leveled well upon his great broad head as he came in a straight line toward me, aiming to put my ball between his eyes. I fired; he fell to his knees. In an instant I saw that it was not a death shot; my ball had struck too high, glancing over, taking off the skin for a couple or more inches, and commenced reloading. The dogs covered him before he rose from the stunning effect of the shot. He had only come to his knees. Cæsar and Bess were to their places, the half-hounds holding him well behind. Several of the dogs had gotten to the front, thinking it was all up with him. Rising upon his rump he made a plunge, but was impeded by the dogs. Cæsar and Bess were fast hold of their favorite catch, close under his deep sides; they were holding on to their part of his broad arms close up to his body. I had moved my position, pressing one side into the cane to his broadside. By this time he had fully recovered from his stun; a large yellow quarter-hound of Pet's was at his head; in attempting to make his escape he was prevented by the cane and became a victim of the monster's great jaws, crushing him through and through close over his vitals. Making another plunge he relieved himself of Cæsar, dashing him against the cane, and broke for the slash. I was just in the act of priming for another shot; a moment more and I would have been the little king bee of the hunt, for he was the "oldest inhabitant" of the woods. The hunters in the slash stood ready for him; he crashed through the cane like a young tornado. Clearing the cane, five well-aimed rifle bullets were shot into him, three passing through his heart. His running being accelerated, he ran across the slash and fell full length upon his broad belly at the head of the clay-gut, with a loud groan or moan, as if human. When we reached him he was dead—dead as he fell. The monster bear, the oldest inhabitant of his kind, the bear that had worried our friend Cary and his dogs so often, the great bear of the Big Hatchie country, of the Big Hurricane, lay dead before us. We spread ourselves out on the ground to rest; tired, though dealing out but little physical toil. The hunter's mind, soul and heart had been in intense excitement till the killing—we were tired from the relax. Cary blowed his horn for the boys; we waited their coming. It gave us time to rest and comment upon the last half hour's work, which our good looking young leader said in the early morning was worth a week's hunting. We had relieved our friend Cary's hunting ground of his two troubles—the great bear and the panther. He was as fat as bear of his size and age ever get to be. Without any means of weighing him, the hunters' estimate as he lay, was that he would weigh a little short of seven hundred pounds. His age, who knew? He had grown gray around the eyes, and his teeth worn off more than half their original length. The writer is, perhaps, the only one living of the hunters in that celebrated hunt, when the big bear of the Big Hurricane was killed. He was then a boy in his thirteenth year; the then youngest of the hunters was his friend Cary, who died several years after. Whether any of the others are among the living is unknown to him; if living, they will testify to the material statements in the account of this hunt—it took place forty-five years ago. If the old negro Jack is living he will bear witness, if the reader thinks the writer is dealing in fiction. Jack was then thirty; he was an old young negro; he was living in Memphis last year. When the boys arrived all hands went to work; some holding, some ripping, and others skinning. The hide was soon stripped from his huge carcass. The five bullet holes were plainly in relief, and each hunter could have claimed his shot from the size of the hole, either one of which would have killed him; a small breakfast plate would have covered them all. Four poles were procured, a quarter put on each, and two men to a pole, we started back down the clay-gut. The hide was assigned to the writer; it was as much as he could possibly carry; more, had he not had a hand in the killing. After much toil we reached the bottom. The two bears killed that morning were more than three horses could pack, so we bent down some saplings and hung up enough for another trip. The boys had plenty time, as the sun had just crossed the meridian.

We all returned to the camp the same way that we came, and spent the afternoon talking over the events and incidents of the morning. A fine, fat gobbler was suspended before the fire, roasting for our dinner.

Reader, did you ever eat of a fat gobbler, a wild one, roasted before the fire? None of you young ones havn't, I guess, for it was a dish for "old times," before cooking stoves were brought into use. Rich, brown and juicy, I have seen them carved at my father's table.

An hour before sundown, the Captain stalked off to roost another gang of turkeys, remarking, that for his eating he wouldn't give one fat turkey for a whole six-hundred-pound bear. No one dissented.

The sunset gave promise of another fair day. The old proverb, that

"Evening red and morning gray
Sets the traveler on his way;
Evening gray and morning red
Brings down rain upon his head,"

is remembered by all old hunters, and relied upon in determining the character of the weather for the next day. We had come to make a three days' hunt, returning Christmas eve. The hunt for the morrow was to be in the Big Bend, below the mouth of the lagoon. The Captain had gone after his turkeys, taking Pete. The hunters whiled away the hour until he returned in camp talk and relating anecdotes. The negroes stood around enjoying the jokes, when old Jack put in and said:

"Mars Cary, has my young hunter master told you 'bout Mistiss and the childen going chestnut hunting, and being most scared to death by the bear?"

"No," said Cary. "How was it, Jack? You tell it."

"Well, you see, Mistiss, she had promised the childen to go wid 'em chestut-hunting. So one Saturday, after dinner, they all went. Mistiss, she took all the white childen and the little darkies to pick up chestnuts. They went down the creek half a mile—mebbe a little more. The chestnut trees was fuller last fall than they has been since we moved to the country. They had just begun to open, but hadn't begun to fall out; so she took me along with my ax to cut down the small trees that was fullest. My young master, there, he went along too. He took his little rifle to shoot squirrels."

"Well, Jack," said Cary, "we want to get to the chestnuts and the bear."

"Ise gwine right thar, Mars Cary, as fast and as straight as I can take you. Well, as I was saying, Mistiss took the white childen and the young darkies"—

"But you have told us that, Jack."

"Well, we will just say that we got to the chestnut trees without going."

"That is it, Jack," said Cary, "go on."

"Well, Mistiss, she and the childen is at the chestnut trees. The childen, they was running about picking up chestnuts; they want plenty on the grown. Mistiss, she was walking about on the high bluff, with a bunch of yellow flowers in her hand; the trees was on the bluff."

"Well, Jack, what about the bear? Where was he?" said Cary.

Well, I declar, Mars Cary, if you aint the most impationest man I ever did see. Aint I getting to the bear part fast as I kin? You see Mistiss, as I said, was walkin on the bluff, and the childen, they was running about after chestnuts; they wasent plenty on the ground."

"But the bear; how did he scare?"

"Well, aint I coming right straight to the bear? As I was saying, the chestnuts want plenty on the ground. They heard em falling thick little ways b'low, and way they went. Mistiss, she was standing on the bluff. She was close by the tree the childen was running to. She just looked up the tree to see if it was full of chestnuts, and she began to scream, and scream as loud as she could, 'bear! bear!' The childen, they began to scream and squall. You never did hear sich screaming. The childen hollard 'where, where?' They was scared so bad they didn't know which way to look or run, till the old bear made such a fuss up the tree, raking the bark as she was backing down. The childen looked up. The bear had got close down to the ground. Her two cubs, just above her, coming down, too. The childen broke for home, Mistiss she right after them, screaming and squalling as they went. The childen and Mistiss hadn't got no ways before the old bear and cubs was on the ground, running like the dogs was after them, the other way. I hollard, and hollard for them to come back, but they wouldn't here me nohow, and they didn't stop till they was home."

"Well, Jack, that is a good one, but where was your young Master with his rifle?"

"Lor bless me, he was under the bluff shootin' squirrels."

Just then the Captain came in; he and Pet loaded with turkeys. He had his seven this time.

Two hours before day all were up, guns shot off, wiped out, re-loaded and primed, and waiting breakfast. We made an early start for the hunting-ground agreed upon. Crossing the lagoon, we were soon in the switch-cane. Before reaching the thick cane, old "Start" struck a running trail. The half-hounds joined him, and they went upon a full run in the direction of the river. The hunters pressed on after them. Temple gave Cæsar and Bess word to "go in." Reaching a wet slash, Cary, who was ahead, stopped to examine the tracks, to see what manner of bear the dogs were after. Coming up to him, he said: "It's an old she and two cubs."

Before leaving the place, we heard the dogs in "full cry," coming as if on the "back track." Cary remarked that they had divided. In another moment Cæsar and Bess, with a couple of the half-hounds, over-reached the cub (he had become seperated from the dam, and was making his way back to where they started), and had him stretched upon the ground. When Cary got up he dispatched him with his knife. The pack were on a "big run" after the old she. She was making her best run to reach the Big Hurricane. Cæsar and Bess, with the half-hounds, were put in after her, fresh from the killing of the cub. They didn't require to be hurried. The hunters hurried; getting to the lagoon, we brought a halt to hear the movement of the dogs. They had her at a lively bay, in the open woods, near the Hurricane. We increased our run for a short distance. Discovering that she had changed her course, Temple remarked that his dogs had headed her off from the Hurricane.

"That will suit Ab," says the Captain, "it well help him to get up to the killing."

She turned in toward the river, heading back for the big bend. We pressed on after them. She was soon brought to a "stop" again. Before we got up, her course was changed in the direction of the camp.

"Well," says the Captain, "we had better save our breath; wait here till she concludes to stop and make fight."

"Cæsar and Bess will keep her angling about in this open woods till we get up in sight. She'll go no further then," said Temple.

"Then," says Ab, "we had better greet them with our presence."

Her course changed again, and she was coming full tilt straight to where we were standing. As she got within gun-shot of us, Cæsar dashed in, swinging her half round. She broke again, when the dog clinched her again. By this time Bess was at her place, and fast hold of the other arm, bringing her upon her all-fours, the half-hounds covering her behind. She made no further efforts to break, and turned upon the dogs. She fought hard and furious. Raising upon her hind legs, she shook her great body like an earthquake, to rid herself of the dog and slut. The dog let go, and she made a terrible effort to get hold of Bess. In a moment the dog renewed his attack, taking her close up to the body, brought her down upon her side. To save himself, he let go. The half-hounds closed in upon her hard and heavy. She rose furious. She had become desperate. Her other arm being free, she made an effort to reach Bess. The slut hung on like "grim death," keeping her body well under the bear. The fight became fearfully terrific, when Cary said:

"The dogs have had enough of it; we will go in and end the fight. Mr. Temple, end the fight, your slut will get hurt."

Temple was of the same opinion. He waited a safe chance and shot her through the heart. She winced under it, staggered around and fell, falling upon the slut. Could Bess have uttered language suited to her feelings, she would have sung:

"We cling to one another until death us do part."

"Well, friend Temple," said Ab, "your dogs seem to be badly worried this time."

"Yes," responded he, "it is always the case when they get hold of an old she that has cubs. The only time the slut was ever badly scratched was by an old she. They always fight harder when the cubs are following them."

"I reckon," said the Captain, "that we ought to be satisfied now. Mr. Temple's dogs have far surpassed anything I could have conceived. They are under better command than any dogs I ever saw, and their handling a bear is unsurpassed. This is our last day's hunt, and I think we ought to stop on this. We have already killed six bears, four of them aggregating more meat than any four bears that was ever slaughtered in these woods."

"Don't forget the turkeys," said Ab; "I counted twelve hanging on the pole this morning—all big gobblers—that will, as you say by the four bears, aggregate in weight more than any twelve gobblers I ever saw."

"Yes;" said the Captain, "we shall have more than the boys can well pack home. We must have at least two thousand pounds of bear meat. I suggest that we end the hunt here; to-morrow will be Christmas, and my friend Ab wouldn't like to miss his egg-nog, and I want my little hunter friend's mother to have a fat gobbler for her Christmas dinner."

It was agreed to end the hunt there. The sun had not crossed the meridian. The hunters assisted the boys with the old she, and we were soon at camp dividing and packing up.

"What is in that big bank of ashes, there?" said Ab to old Jack.

"Why, its Mr. Temple's barr feet. He put 'em in dis mornin', and told us to mine 'em and keep 'em covered up; I spec deys dun, now."

"Yes," said Temple; "I wanted a good mess of

bear feet before we left the camp. Jack, are they done, do you think?"

"Yes, sir; Ise been smellin' dem some time. I knows dey is done."

"Pull them out, then," said Temple. "Mind, don't let the hair scorch."

Jack rolled out a couple of large paws, roasted in the ashes to a smoking done. The ashes brushed off clean, Temple forked one up, stripped off the skin, which slipped off like peeling a roasted onion, and a more delicate morsel was never greeted by man's appetite. None but a bear-hunter knows how to roast a bear's paw; the fore feet are the best. The writer can testify to their eating qualities. Everything being packed, the hunters parted with expressions of mutual gratification.

CHAPTER VI.

Lawyers Riding the Circuit—The Methodist Preacher—The Scalding Cup of Coffee—The Nation's Muster—Bloody Noses and Black Eyes—Proposed Prize Fight—Ab and the Squatter's Wife—John Smith and Daniel Parker.

THE only place for man and beast to find rest, between Brownsville and Covington, was at my father's house. He turned no one away. It was the habit, in those days, for the lawyers to "ride the circuit," to attend all the courts in the judicial district in which they resided. The lawyers of Jackson and Brownsville practiced in the Circuit Court at Covington, attending regularly the fall and spring terms.

Among the early practitioners were Haskell, Bradford and Huntsman, of Jackson, and Loving, Strother and Richmond, of Brownsville.

JOSHUA HASKELL

was the first Circuit Court Judge in West Tennessee. Tall and good looking, with great respect for his personal, his manner and mein marked him as a type of a well-finished gentleman. When on the bench, he commanded the high respect of the bar; maintaining, with propriety, the dignity due his high and honored position. Many incidents and anecdotes occurring in the practice of the courts, at that early period, are still preserved. I am indebted to one of the "Old Folks"—the oldest of them all—perhaps the only surviving cotemporary of that period, for the following incident that occurred during the first court held by Judge Haskell in Dyer county.

The court was held in 'Squire Warren's dwelling-house, in the winter of 1823–4. The house was a common double log cabin, one end of which was occupied by the family. There were only three cases on the docket. A "log-heap" fire was built outside to make comfortable and warm those in attendance upon the court, who were not on the jury. 'Squire Warren was on the jury. A trading boat had landed at Cherry's bluff, on the Forked Deer, from which a supply of whisky had been obtained by the neighbors, a portion of which had found its way to the 'Squire's house, and was circulating freely around the "log-heap" fire, as well as among those in the temporary court-room; and as the boys grew warm under the influence of both *fires*, a dispute arose between Berry Nash and a son of the proprietor, young Tom Warren. The quarrel culminated in blows. Berry let fly at young Tom, and Tom gave back blow for blow. The old 'Squire had a view from the jury box, through the cracks of the logs, of what was going on around the "log-heap" fire. Becoming excited himself, he hallooed out at the top of his voice to his son, "Hit him again Tom, hit him! Never let it be said that a man hit you on your own dunghill, and you didn't hit him back!" Tom, hearing the admonition of the old man, went into the fight in earnest, and badly "used up" Berry. The Judge—permitting the fight to go on until it was ended—ordered the Sheriff, Charley McCrarey, to bring the two young men into court. Nash, the aggressor, was the first brought in, a fine assessed, and the Sheriff ordered to keep him in custody until it was paid. Young Warren was then called up before the court, and the Judge was in the act of pronouncing a fine against him, when the old 'Squire rose from his seat among the jurors, and said:

"Stop, stop, Judge; I'd naturally like to hear the law read that fines a man for fighting on his own dunghill!"

The late William R. Hess, a lawyer in attendance, and who was a friend to both parties, rose, and proclaimed that there was no such law, and suggested, as the easiest way to settle the matter, that the young men go to the branch, wash their faces, come back and take a drink, make friends and go home. The jury had become so much demoralized by the *rumpus*, that the Judge ordered the Sheriff to adjourn court, with the admonition, that if the people of Dyer county did not do better the next time he held court, he would put the heads of all offenders "under the fence." Judge Haskell contributed greatly to the merriment of the lawyers and lovers of fun in their journeying around the circuit. He enjoyed a good joke.

ALEXANDER B. BRADFORD,

a handsome young lawyer, was the most attractive

of the lawyers that rode the circuit. Dressing well, he was ever clothed in a finely fitting suit of fine blue broadcloth, with bright buttons. He seemed to have been born in the habiliments of style—a very Chesterfield in manners and address. A great favorite with my mother, he paid her the most courtly respect; a warm personal friend of the family, he was ever a welcome guest at my father's house. General Bradford was among the earliest and first lawyers of West Tennessee, and was intimately connected and associated with the practice and jurisprudence of West Tennessee from the organizing of the first courts, running through a period of more than a quarter of a century. The mention of his name thrills the bosom of all who knew him and enjoyed his personal acquaintance, as a very *type of a true man.* An old-young lawyer was

MAJOR RICHMOND.

A wit and humorist, everybody enjoyed his society. He wore fine clothes, and kept his fur hat smooth by a habit of using his coat sleeve for a brush. The Major was gifted with a fund of anecdote; for the most part original, but not admissible in polite reading. He was the leading lawyer in "road cases." He used to say of himself, that he was "h—l upon roads." He was sought for and employed in all "divorce cases," and was the best *crim. con.* lawyer in the district.

GENERAL LOVING

was the idol of the bar in the early history of the courts at Brownsville. His personal was unexceptionable and faultless, both in form, manner and features. His name merits a high place in the annals and history of Haywood.

JOHN W. STROTHER, ESQ.,

was the lawyer among the lawyers of Brownsville in the early practice of the courts. Thin in flesh, wiry in nerve and tissue, and careless of dress and the personal, he passed among strangers for less than he "was worth." For more than a quarter of a century he lived in Brownsville. With great gentleness of manner, and purity of heart, he enjoyed a reputation worthy the strict sobriety and purity of his conduct.

The party of lawyers, with the Judges, stopped at my father's house to stay all night, on their way to the Covington court. It was the spring term. I remember that it was "gobbling season," when the bark of the young hickory begins to slip. It was Saturday evening. It was the aim of the lawyers to reach Covington Sunday evening, before Monday, the first day of court. They were in no hurry for breakfast; it being Sunday morning, nobody was in a hurry. All nature enjoys sweet repose in the soft mornings of spring, and all hands "and the cook" are licensed to sleep late on Sunday mornings in the country.

Breakfast was ready and waiting for the guests, when a couple of strangers rode up and asked for breakfast and horse-feed. My father told them to get down and come in, ordering their horses to be taken and fed. The breakfast was on the table;

their coming delayed its being served up until they had washed their hands and faces. They had the appearance of having laid out all night, but were well dressed in broadcloth. On their coming in one of them introduced himself, and then introduced his traveling companion as the Reverend Mr. Hutchington. (The reverend part need not have been introduced, as all who were familiar with the fashions of the day knew from the cut of his coat, which was a regular shad-belly, that he was a Methodist preacher.)

Breakfast was announced, and they were invited to seats at the table. My father, it was ever his custom, said grace—his every day grace: "Lord bless us in what we are about to receive, for Christ's sake."

The reverend gentleman, as he raised his head, threw a glancing eye upon the head of the family as he finished his short blessing, as much as to say: "My professional calling is not recognized."

Helping and changing of plates went on from a large dish of turkey steak (which was common with us, as it was only a walk across the field to take down a gobbler any morning during "gobbling season.")

Coffee, an article of luxury in those days, was dished out and passed around. My mother, ever mindful of her North Carolina raising, showed the agreeable, commencing with the nearest guest:

"Judge Haskell, is your coffee agreeable?"

"Thank you, Madam, most agreeable. Such a cup of coffee I have not tasted in the district."

"Do you take cream in your coffee, Major Richmond?"

"If you please, Madam."

"Colonel Bradford, I neglected to ask you if your coffee was agreeable."

"Madam, it is nectar itself." Smacking his lips, he continued in its praise until my father had to remind him that it would get cold. Passing around with like questions, she came to the preacher and said:

"And you, sir, is your coffee agreeable?"

"Yes, Madam, only it's a *little cold.*"

Major Richmond's quizzical eye was upon him in an instant, and then at my mother, who was dumb.

The reverend gentleman, thinking that *truth* was the propriety of language *at all times*, braved the cutting of eyes across the table. He may have aimed an arrow for not being called upon to "ask a blessing."

To relieve the situation, which had been *chilled* a little by the cup of "cold coffee," the humorous Major, addressing himself to the Parson, inquired where he and his friend had stayed all night.

"On the river-bank, sir," he replied, "with the sand-beach for a pillow. We reached the ferry after night-fall. The ferryman had left. After splitting our throats hallooing for him, we made our couch upon the sand."

"Then you must have a pretty good appetite this morning," said the Major.

"Yes, sir. We rode all day, not eating anything since yesterday at breakfast, and a poor one it was."

Just then his "cold cup" was out. My mother asked him if he would have another cup of coffee. He thanked her, at the same time sending up his cup.

In the meantime a fresh pot of coffee had been brought in, scalding hot, from which she filled his cup and returned it. The Major having him engaged in a lively talk, he had not observed it smoking; thinking it was like its predecessor, or possibly colder still, he raised it to his lips and took a hearty sip, filling his mouth full of the scalding fluid. (*Gimeny!*) So unexpected, unable to turn right or left without scalding his neighbor, he let fly, the coffee gushing out of his mouth like an inch and a half squirt gun all over the table. Not waiting to be asked if his coffee was "agreeable," he rose from the table with his bandanna to his mouth, and made for the water pail.

"Well," said his traveling companion, who seemed not to sympathize with him, "my reverend friend has got a touch of the *blue blazes* this time; wonder if he wont prefer it cold next time?"

The breakfast closed with the Parson's second cup of coffee. The jolly Major followed him out to the water pail condoling with him, for he was terribly scalded. My mother soon followed with a cup of new cream, offering a thousand apologies for not informing him that she had filled his cup from a fresh pot, and explaining how it was that his first cup was cold, pressing upon him to take a mouthful of *cold cream*, that it would alleviate his suffering; she was so sorry, regretted so much the mishap, and hoped that he would soon be well of it. The incident of the Methodist preacher, and the hot cup of coffee, was ever remembered by the party present on that Sabbath morning, and served as an amusing topic for many years afterward.

The settlements north of the Big Hatchie, in Tipton, had began to form voting precincts and organize the militia. A battalion muster was to come off that spring at Hurricane Hill. A *big muster* in those days attracted every one; the old, who had *passed muster*, as well as the under age; men, women, children and negroes gathered at a muster. Cakes and pies, with beer and cider, was always on hand in thick profusion; not unfrequently a barrel of "red-eye" was found on tap under the hill near the spring. The drum and fife (no company was allowed to be mustered in without its drum and fife Major) was music most divine, bringing out the most thrilling patriotic demonstrations. The drum and the fife, to the tune of "Yankee Doodle" and the "Jay bird died with the whooping cough," failed not to arouse the "spread eagle" in everybody's bosom—glorious days was "old times." General Jackson, the military chieftain of the age, was the rising man for the Presidency; the eighth of January was yet fresh in the land; a military parade was most *enthusing*; it was the sovereign's day, a *nation's muster*. The settlements all turned out to the *big muster* at Hurricane Hill that day. The gathering of the denizens culminated early. The Lieutenants, with their drummers, had taken their positions to form. From half a dozen hillocks, or shady places, was heard:

"Oh yes! oh yes! all who belong to Captain Jones' company will fall into ranks."

"Oh yes! oh yes! Captain Barnes' company will form; fall into ranks."

"Oh yes! oh yes! Captain Smith's company will fall into ranks." Thus went the rounds until the different companies composing the battalion were formed. Then commenced the drilling:

"Eyes right, and dress! Shoulder arms! Order arms! *Drop your butts square upon the ground, with the cocks behind!* Keep your left arms straight down your left leg. Now, shoulder arms!" Thus the drill continued until mustered off by the Adjutant Major and formed into battalion, and marched out to the field for further manœuvering according to "Scott's tactics."

The *mustering* over, the battalion was marched back to the store and disbanded, when a rush was made for the cake and beer stands, many finding their way to the barrel of "red-eye" on tap under the hill. As the day began to wane, the *spirit* of the "critter" began to brew the usual fights. A squad of jolly fellows made a raid on one of the pie and cake stands, lead by the "Bully of the Hill," Ab Gaines. Gaines had gotten hold of the young vendor of the pies and cakes by the nap of his neck, handling him roughly—thumping his head against the cake stand—while his chums were filling their pockets. John Barnes, the blacksmith, was standing near, and being a friend to the young man, beside an advocate of fair play, he remonstrated with the "Bully of the Hill." Gaines resented the interference in a menacing manner, when Barnes *let drive*, sprawling him upon the ground, with the remark: "You coward; you have *bullied this Hill long enough!*" Ab rose to his feet and "went for" Barnes, making a pass. Barnes was too quick for him, and Ab went to the ground again. In the meantime the friends of the parties had began to close in and around. The writer, yet in his early teens, mounted the cake stand to get out of the way, and to obtain a better view of the fight. Gaines rose to his feet again, cried "fair play," and went at Barnes the third time, when a well placed blow, over his left temple and eye, brought him to the ground harder than ever. A general fight had begun; a dozen or more men were having a regular "set-to." None attempted to interfere or part them; eyes and noses were suffering terribly; they fought on until "each man had whipped his man." Ab was the first to propose a truce. With difficulty he arose to his feet after the third knock-down, and said:

"You are more than a match for me to-day. I am not in a fix to fight to-day. I am drunk; too drunk to hold you a good fight. I'll see you again."

"You can see me whenever it may suit you. I take no advantage of a drunken man. I will meet you in a 'square fight' whenever it may please you to name the time and place," said Barnes.

"It had as well be on this Hill, and this day two weeks; I will be here with my friends," said Gaines.

"It suits me," said Barnes; "name the hour.

"Let it be an hour to sunset," responded Gaines.

"I'll be here," said Barnes, when he separated himself from the crowd.

The interest taken in the coming "square fight," between two of the most powerful men in the settlement, had caused the other belligerents to forget their differences. Black eyes and bloody noses only remained to give evidence of the bloody "set-to" that had just occurred. All hands made friends, took a drink, and went home.

It was soon *norrated* through the settlement that Ab Gaines and John Barnes were to have a "square fight;" that the bully of Hurricane Hill had found his match. It was a matter of much surprise, however, to the sober, steady men of the neighborhood that a man of Barnes' steady habits should enter the list of prize fighters. It was agreed, however, that Ab needed taking down, and no man could be found better able to do it than Barnes. Gaines was the heaviest man of the two; he stood full six feet five, broad and deep through the chest, and wore a number eleven shoe; and a hand—it was difficult to find a glove large enough to fit. Barnes, less in pounds and inches, was greatly his superior in the material of flesh, *tissue and muscle.* Made more powerful by hard licks at the anvil, he had never failed in an enterprise or undertaking dependent upon his manhood.

Time was required for Ab to work the mean whisky out of him, and reduce himself in flesh. Could he do it? was the grave question among his intimate friends. Their coming together upon equal advantages was fearful to contemplate. Barnes' courage was undoubted; Gaines had played the bully, but had never sought his match; it was doubted whether he had the courage of his adversary in the coming conflict. As the time drew nigh for them to meet, it was whispered through the neighborhood that Ab was *softening*—that he would "flicker." Bets were being freely offered that he wouldn't come to time, and found no takers. His friends began to rally him; the boasting and big talk on their part had "dried up." Ab, through the aid of his friends, had well nigh gotten the whisky out of himself, and cheered on to the conflict, when, a few days before the appointed day, he, with several of his friends, were at the Hill, and he got a *taste* of whisky. He tasted often, and drank deep; his friends could do nothing with him. In their efforts to keep him from drinking too much, he "let fly" with that great fist of his and smashed several of their noses, and they left him to his fate. They had gone before he discovered that he was alone. With some difficulty he got on his horse and started for home. In going home he had to pass a *squatter* settler's house situated on the roadside. When getting near the *squatter's* house, he observed a man *flailing* a woman in the front yard. Spurring up his horse, he went to her rescue. The *squatter* had his wife by the hair of her head, slinging her around, when Ab took hold of him, jerking him loose from his hold upon her hair and flat of his back, and commenced pounding him heavily in the face. The wife, freed from the rough handling of her husband, turned upon Gaines. Seizing an ax that lay near, she sent it into his back up to the eye, leaving it sticking in him, with the remark: "Now, let my husband alone." Ab rolled off the *squatter*, crying out, "Murder! murder!"

The husband rose to his feet and pulled the ax out of his back, when the rush of blood was most fearful. Mounting Ab's horse, he rode for the nearest doctor as fast as he could, who was soon in attendance, and examined the fearful cut. The ax had gone in over the region of the liver, severing one or more ribs, and cutting off a portion of the liver, which the Doctor took out. The bleeding was profuse, and the Doctor pronounced it fatal.

"There is no hope for you, Ab," he said; "the bleeding is internal and can't be stanched. If you have any worldly affairs about which you want to leave instructions, it will be well that you go about it."

"I have none," said Gaines. "Only one request will I make. You say there is no hope; then my last request is, that you will send up to the store and get me a gallon of whisky."

"You shall have it, Ab," replied the Doctor.

The squatter, with the aid of his wife and the Doctor, got Ab in the house, and fixed a pallet on the floor. He then rode to the store for the whisky. The Doctor remained until the squatter returned with the jug of whisky. A tin cup was provided, and Ab told to drink at his pleasure.

The Doctor left him with his comforter, saying that he would ride over the next morning.

The next day, to the astonishment of the Doctor,

he found Ab alive, and the jug empty. He finally recovered, but was never himself again. The apology for not meeting Barnes in a test of manhood at the "Hill" on the following Saturday was satisfactory.

About this time the *upper settlement* was enjoying the relative merits of the manhood of John Smith and Daniel Parker. Both of them being quiet, good neighbors, and regular attendants at church, they startled the neighborhood by a *falling out.* A cotemporary of "old times," on the Big Lagoon, relates the occurrence to me in this wise:

Smith engaged Parker to dig him a well. The price for digging it was agreed upon. According to Smith's words, Parker would find water in thirty feet, and the price to be paid was twenty-five ears of corn per foot, which would be seven bushels and a half. Corn was then selling at two dollars per bushel. The bargain was made in the spring of the year. Parker was to go to work right away, and to take one-half of the number in *roasting-ears,* as soon as Smith's corn was old enough. Parker was slow in commencing the job, digging all through the roasting-ear season, taking home with him every night as many roasting-ears as his day's labor would come to. His family was large, and it was their only bread. The digging continued until the depth of thirty feet had been reached. The corn, in the meantime, had got hard; Parker continuing, however, to take his twenty or more ears home every night, which would be *grated* and bread made of it. By the time the thirty feet was reached Parker had taken up three hundred or more ears, and had not come to water, and, from the signs, was not likely to find it in perhaps thirty feet more of digging. A "water witch" had, with his "witch-hazle" twig, located the place for digging the well, and given *his* guarantee to Smith that water would be found in thirty feet from the surface. Smith's faith in the mystic art had induced him to name thirty feet as the distance Parker would have to dig to find water. The average wells of the neighborhood were sixty feet, and Parker declined digging any deeper unless he got an increased number of ears of corn per foot. Smith was not willing to accord it, and the digging stopped. Smith was excitable by nature, a man of immense size in flesh, and the heaviest man in the neighborhood by an hundred pounds. He vowed, and swore he would stand by it, that if Parker didn't continue digging until he found water, he should not have another ear of corn. Parker, whose frame of bones was capable of carrying more flesh than Smith's did, the largest *raw-bony* man in the settlement, and with all an acknowledged good fighter, swore that if Smith didn't let him have the number of ears due him on the digging, he would whip it out of him. Smith was firm and Parker resolute. They soon met. It was on *road-working* day, where all the neighborhood had gathered to work on the road. Each party had their friends, and the fight was to be a fair one; no interference until Parker had whipped his two hundred and fifty ears of corn out of Smith, if he should prefer that kind of a settlement. Smith announced that he was willing to that kind of a settlement, if it would satisfy Parker, when he got through. So at it they went, stripped to their shirts. Smith was amiable in standing fair for Parker's blows, making it his aim to keep them out of his face and eyes, showing himself an adept in fencing off the well aimed blows at his head and face. Parker, becoming a little weary in his futile effort in that direction, commenced his heavy *digs* in Smith's short ribs, and what he conceived to be the tender place, about the pit of his stomach, belaboring himself in using first one fist and then the other, until he was well nigh exhausted. In the meantime Smith's friends yelled out that Parker ought to be satisfied, when Parker, becoming good natured all at once, declared himself satisfied, saying that he would as soon undertake to fight a bag of feathers.

"And," says Smith, "I would as soon undertake to strike at a horn-beam stump."

CHAPTER VII.

The Character of the Men who Settled West Tennessee—Tipton County, its Original Territory and Topographical Features—Organization and Officers of the First Courts—The First Venire of Grand and Petit Juries—Jacob Tipton—Robert Sanford—Covington—The first Merchants—The First Physicians—The Calmes Tavern—The Tavern-Keeper—The Boys about Town—The New Sign and the Bell-Ringing—The Calves in the Court-House—Holnhouser's Court—Old Johnny Giddins—Tacket Kills Mitchell—Gray Case; his Life Staked upon a Game of Cards—Rufus Garland—Grandville D. Searcy—The Fourth of July Celebration—Charles G. Fisher—Nathan Adams—William Coward and the Wolf Story—Armstead Morehead—David Crockett and his Competitors for Congress.

It was not from the cesspools and scum of the society of old States that West Tennessee was peopled. The rich and fertile virgin lands of the district early attracted the enterprising and industrious men of wealth and intelligence, the strongest and best material from the old States—a historic fact well attested by many now living who have kept pace with "ever marching time."

The brave hearts and strong arms of the heroic fathers, husbands and sons were nobly sustained by the heroism of their wives, mothers and daughters, who shared with them the toils and hardships of subduing the wilderness.

Oh, ye daughters of sunshine and ease! ye lovely women of romance and pleasure! ye dwellers in the gay "social solitude!" ye revelers in the fashions of gay city life, delicate exotics of a soft, luxuriant society! think of the noble, brave-hearted mothers, wives and daughters who triumphantly battled against the perils and hardships of a frontier life, aiding and encouraging their husbands, fathers, sons and brothers in subduing the forests and opening up the wildwoods, making it the fitting abode for refined civilized enjoyment. Noble mothers! Fond memories of their heroism are embalmed in the heart's affection, the common heritage of their successors.

The eye of the traveler when passing through West Tennessee of the present day is amazed with pleasurable delight in seeing its broad acres teeming with wealth and luxury, with its beautifully built cities and towns, its lovely resident mansions and refined and elegant society, and wonders when told that it is all the *growth of less than half a century;* that of the early settlers, who came with the pocket-compass in their hands, followed by the blazer with his ax, many are yet among the active men of the present day—are yet living to recount where the first "corner-stone" was laid, and point to where the first tent was pitched in the wilderness. The limits of these reminiscences, however, is restricted alone to the past, to "old times," and it is of Tipton and Covington that I would write in this chapter.

It was not until the year 1818 that the Chickasaw

title to the lands west of the Tennessee river, within the limits of the State, was extinguished. The year following, 1819, by an act of the Legislature, the territory known as the Big Hatchie country was attached for judicial purposes to the county of Hardin. In 1821, by the act fixing the boundaries of Madison and Shelby, the territory forming the county of Tipton was attached to Shelby, until 1823, when it became a separate and independent county, and the boundaries established.

Bordering on the Mississippi river to the west, to the north and south by the waters of the Forked Deer and Loosa Hatchie, with the Big Hatchie running through the center, no county in the State could boast of so rich a body of virgin lands, or offered such inducements to the enterprising agriculturist. The topographical features of the county differ but little from the other counties in West Tennessee, noted only for its beautiful western front, overlooking the great river. The "Mill Stone Mountain," an interesting feature, found among the range of hills bordering on the Big Hatchie, near its mouth—a novelty of itself—is the more interesting for its being a solid mass of concrete rock, from which is wrought the best mill-stones in use; said to be equal, if not better, than the celebrated French burr. Less than a half mile in diameter at its base, it rises in cone shape from the banks of the Hatchie, towering above the tallest forest trees, its apex perfectly level, overlooking the surrounding country. Above and near it, on the banks of the Hatchie, is a well marked ancient fortification, from the foot-prints of time judged to belong to the period when the "Mound Race" inhabited the country. The location seems to have been well taken, in an abrupt bend of the river, and constructed after the manner of constructing fortifications in modern days; in the ditch forming a crescent towards the land-front, numerous forest trees are growing of huge size, in age apparently equal to the oldest in the forest. Within the fortification are several "mounds," from which human bones have been taken, with specimens of pottery or earthen ware. It is related to the writer, by a descendant of one of the oldest and first settlers in Tipton, that many years ago a fragment of a well burnt brick was picked up in the vicinity of this ancient fortification, upon which the foot-print of a goat was well defined. To *suppose* about it, would be that the goat left his foot-print upon the brick while lying upon the yard, and before it was put into the kiln to be burnt. In the same vicinity, many feet below the surface of the earth, charcoal and charred pieces of wood have been dug up. That brickbat, as well as the old fortification with its connecting history, must be left to the pen of the curious, who may assume to write of the period beyond the dark ages; of an extinct race whose only history is left in the silent tombs of their own making, possibly before Noah was called upon to lay the keel and temper the ribs of the ark.

It is of Tipton and the first settlers under the dominion of the State of Tennessee that I write.

On the first day of December, 1823, the first court was organized and held at the house of Nathan

Hartsfield, two or more miles southwest of where Covington now stands. It was organized and held by the first magistrates appointed for the county by Governor Carroll, and were Nathan Hartsfield, John T. Brown, Jacob Tipton, Andrew Greer, John C. McKean and George Robinson. John C. McKean was made chairman of the court. The court being organized, they went into an election for county officers, which resulted as follows:

Andrew Greer, Clerk; John T. Brown, Sheriff; Nathan Hartsfield, Register; William Henson, Ranger; George Robinson, Coroner. It may be observed that the members of the court elected themselves to the first offices of the county. We are not to conclude, however, that it was for the emoluments, but for the lack of material in men to fill them. It is mentioned as an instance of the sparseness of the inhabitants of the county, that in that year the first wedding took place, and every white family in the county was invited, and when gathered together the male adults numbered not more than sixty.

It may not be uninteresting to the readers of Old Times in Tipton, to read over the first *venire* from which the petit and grand jurors were chosen for the first courts held in the county after the organization, on the first of December, 1823. They were Owen Evans, Samuel P. Givens, Matthew Isaacs, Matthew Alexander, Alexander Robinson, Daniel Young, William Wright, William Henson, John Smith, N. Elliot, G. Yarbrough, Clarke Burdsall, M. Hutchinson, William Robinson, Samuel Robinson, A. R. Logan, Jubilee Gagin, G. Kenney, John

Robinson, Jefferson Childress and Addison D. Packston. Of these names, including the members and officers, none are now among the living. In 1824 the county site was located at

COVINGTON,

and in 1825 the town was laid off, and the lots sold at public sale, on the twelfth day of April of that year, by commissioners appointed by the court. The commissioners were Marcus Calmes, John Eckford, Robert G. Green, E. T. Pope and Alexander Robinson. Covington is beautifully situated on an eminence overlooking the surrounding range of hills. Within a stone's throw of the public square gushes a bold spring, capable of affording water for a populous city, beside numerous smaller ones of excellent water. The town, when located and established as the county site, was near the center of the county, which comprised a large and fertile territory north of the Big Hatchie. In 1836 the county of Lauderdale was established, leaving Tipton alone south of the Hatchie, and Covington within six miles of its northern boundary.

The county was called for the gallant Jacob Tipton, who was killed while leading his men in a charge against the Indians, near Fort Washington, under command of General St. Clair, in 1791. History* mentions that when the intrepid Captain was on the eve of moving with his command to the support of General St. Clair, and after he had mounted his horse, he rode back in hearing of his wife, and left with her, as his last request, that if he should be

*Ramsey.

killed in the perilous service he was about entering, to change the name of their youngest son, who had been named Armsted Blevins, to Jacob. (Not William, as is mentioned in Ramsey's history. The writer is enabled to make this correction by authority of the immediate family of the late General Tipton.) On the fourth of November, 1791, the brave Captain was killed, and his last injunction to his wife was complied with, and Armsted Blevins became Jacob; the late General Jacob Tipton, among the first and most prominent settlers in Tipton county. He was appointed to the clerkship of the Circuit Court upon its organization in the county, which office he filled for many years. One of nature's noblemen, he was noted for his kind and generous hospitalities and courteous mien. A good and true man, his long and useful life was spent where he first settled, breathing his last midst his family and numerous friends in the old homestead. His name and his noble life fills an honored page in the early history of Tipton county.

ROBERT SANFORD

succeeded to the office of Clerk of the Circuit Court of Tipton. He was called from the plow-handle, and learned to handle the pen in the Clerk's office as deputy clerk. He soon became master of the situation, conducting the office with such marked intelligence and business precision that it was not long before he became the *de facto* Clerk. He was continued in the office by the votes of his fellow-citizens for many long years. Living to a ripe old age, highly esteemed and venerated, he was gathered to his fathers, and sleeps among the tombs of his deceased cotemporaries.

Covington had its steady, sober—always sober—men, beside its frolicsome and rolicsome boys. Among the early settlers and merchants of the place was Major Armsted Morehead. The Major, after a residence of more than a quarter of a century, fixed his residence in the vicinity of Memphis, where he still resides, honored and esteemed as an honest, upright man. For twenty odd years he has supplied annually the market of Memphis with choice watermelons of his own raising; having reached his three-score and ten years, he is yet found, as always heretofore, driving his own team.

Marcus Calmes owned and kept the only tavern in Covington. He had been elected Sheriff of the county; the duties of the office conflicting with his tavern keeping, he offered to sell or lease his tavern.

Good schools had been established in Covington. My father had decided to move there to educate his children. It was suggested to him that he had made reputation among the lawyers, riding the circuits, for feeding "man and beast;" that he would do well to lease Calmes' tavern, and make money while his children were going to school. Obtaining my mother's consent for him to become a tavern-keeper in Covington, he entered upon his new enterprise.

THE OLD LOG TAVERN,

situated on the north side of the public square in Covington, is, or was, standing a few years ago. It was built in 1824 or '25, of hewed logs, sixty feet long by twenty wide; two stories high; a frame shed in the rear its full length, and a broad front gallery, with sleeping apartments overhead, containing ten rooms, including the dining room and ball room. The ball room was large, and when a press of guests came in, it was filled with cots and beds, which only occurred when court was in session, or on the occasion of a general muster. My father entered earnestly upon the duties of tavern-keeping, entertaining all the travelers and many boarders. Covington soon began to be a thriving village, with brick stores and handsomely built frame dwellings, painted white, with green blinds. Its first settlers were of the first families from the old States and Middle Tennessee. The rich, fertile lands of the county invited wealth and enterprise. Among the leading merchants of Covington were Booker, Clarkston, Holmes, Adams, Clarke, Smith and Morehead. The doctors were Stone, Green, Fisher, Hall, David Taylor and Woodward Cook, the latter a capital good fiddler. Old Dr. Cook was a great favorite with the boys and all lovers of good music. The practice of physic was an after-thought with him. The lawyers were Robert G. Green, Tom Taylor 'an old bachelor,' and Grandville D. Searcy, young and sprightly. Phil Glen and Yankee White were added to the list a few years after.

The Methodists, Presbyterians and Baptists had good churches. In those days everybody went to church on Sundays. It was a great day for the exhibition of gallantry and finery. A young man felt lonely in going to church without a young lady swinging to his left arm.

No town or village in the western district had better schools at that time than Covington. The Reverend Doctor Chapman long connected with, and late the President of Chapel Hill, North Carolina, filled a high place both in the church and educational department. His family was an acquisition to the society of Covington.

Among the men of wealth and personal merit, who early settled in the vicinity of Covington, were the Tiptons, Dunhams, Garlands, Browns, Robersons, Hills, Harpers, Pryors, Lauderdales, Cowards, Cottons, Taylors, and many others whose names are identified with the early settlement of the Big Hatchie country—connecting the past with the present.

Covington was not without its dancing master in those days. Who of us, who were young then, who learned how to "forward and back—one—two —three—four and five, and back to place, swing corners and balance all," that don't remember old man Chapman, the dancing master, and his tall and handsome son Gary?

Christmas, New Year's Day, the Eighth of January, Twenty-Second of February and the Fourth of July never passed without a big ball, and no town was without its dancing master, as well as preacher. No store was considered to be well stocked with goods without silk stockings and dancing pumps. "Old times" in Covington were her best days.

Of the early settlers of Covington but few are among the living at this writing.

DR. CHARLES G. FISHER,

among the earliest settlers, has survived all of his cotemporaries. He still resides in the place—residing in the same house that he built more than forty years ago. He was a practicing physician in my father's family forty-five years ago. His long and useful life will entitle his name to a memorial window in every household in and around Covington as one of the fathers of the land.

Of the merchants who were then in active business life, now among the survivors of that early period, whose eventful career comes down to this present writing, none is deserving more of honorable mention than

NATHAN ADAMS.

I remember well his first appearance in Covington. Young and handsome, (he was so regarded by the fair young women), with glossy black hair; intelligent, bewitching dark eyes; always handsomely dressed, with artistically tied cravat. I thought him the very model of a refined, well-dressed gentleman. When the annals and history of West Tennessee shall be written, his name will merit a high place in the pages of her progress, in both city and country. Verging to a ripe old age, having passed his three score years, he yet moves with the elasticity of thirty years ago. A man of progress, an able financier, he now ranks among the wealthy, enterprising men of Memphis. Possessing a refined and appreciative taste, he enjoys life in the circle of his many friends.

Among the cotemporary early settlers in Tipton, now living, and whose name has been identified with the local interest of the country for near a half century, none is more worthy of mention than

WILLIAM COWARD, ESQUIRE.

"Starting in the world a poor boy," he began life in Jackson, Madison county, 1824–5, with Amour & Lake, clerking and running keel boats down the Forked Deer and Mississippi, carrying cotton to New Orleans, they trusting to his integrity to bring back the proceeds. In 1826 he took a look at Memphis, when it was a village at the mouth of Wolf. Aiming to be a tiller of the soil, the rich lands of Tipton attracted him to where he settled in the woods near Covington. He still lives where he first settled, and in the house he first built, where, by his industry and probity, he has amassed a large fortune. Believing in the old adage, "that a rolling stone gathers no moss," he has never sought new places, or engaged in new enterprises. Wm. Coward always has a dollar to lend, and none knows better how to lend it, or who to lend it to. Approaching three-score and ten years, he is yet an active business man, looking after and turning over his honest gains. It is not inappropriate to relate an occurrence that happened in his early life, illustrative of his care and vigil over what belongs to him. He went to New Orleans, with the first crop of cotton he made in Tipton, bringing back the proceeds in hard money in his saddle-bags. Arriving at Randolph, he swung the saddle-bags containing this "hard cash" accross his shoulder and started on foot for home, twelve or fourteen miles distant. Night overtook him soon after leaving the settlement near

Randolph, having many miles of wilderness to pass through. When passing through the most unfrequented portion of it, he was attacked by a hungry pack of wolves. Several miles distant from any house or settlement, with nothing to defend himself but his hickory walking-stick, he was forced to take refuge in the nearest tree. Luckily, a small bending oak was at hand, and up it he went, to where a large limb grew straight up. Finding the weight of his saddle-bags too great to climb the limb with it on his shoulder, he swung it on the first limb and pulled himself above it. The hungry wolves, in their furious attack, would run up on the bending portion of the tree. Finding they could not reach him, they commenced snapping at the bag of hard cash. To keep the hungry beasts from rending the saddle-bags and spilling out all the money, Coward would swing himself down, holding on with one hand while laraping them over the head with his hickory stick. Thus he was kept up the tree defending and keeping the wolves off of his saddle-bags until relieved by daylight, when the hungry wolves left for their dark holes.

The Calmes tavern had no sign indicating that it was a place of entertainment for travelers, other than a horse-rack in front for them to hitch their horses. An expert sign-painter came along, and pursuaded my father to have a fine sign painted and swung up. The suggestion met with favor, and the sign-painter went to work upon a four by four square board. At my mother's suggestion, the name "tavern" was dropped, and "hotel" adopted. "Covington" was painted in the form of a crescent, in large letters, a star in the middle, and "hotel" below, gilded with gold; the ground was blue, bespangled with brilliants. The sign, swung high up in a frame upon a large post painted white, was a credit to the painter, recommending him favorably to the town. For several days it was the attractive point for the boys. Covington had a hotel! A bell was then added to the hotel, put up in a neat belfry on top of the building; which was another attractive point with the boys. Covington could boast of its rolicsome, frolicsome boys, as well as other towns. Hardly a week passed without recording some of their innocent deviltry, such as changing sign boards, etc. Holmes & Adams would walk into their store of a morning under Booker & Clarkson's sign; it was only the trouble of changing them back again. One morning all the milkmaids were running over town inquiring if any one had seen such and such a calf. One "with red sides and white back and belly;" another "with spots all over it, and white in the face." The cows filled the streets lowing their utmost. The town was about to go to breakfast without milk in its coffee, when, from the lowing of the cows, a calf was heard to bleat in the court-house. In the meantime, the inquiries as to the missing calves becoming general, the town folk began to gather on the public square. The cows, hearing the bleating of the calf in the court-house, gathered around it, and the calves set up a unanimous bleating in the court room. The milk women and the boys (who didn't know anything about it) opened the court-house door, and the calves came jumping out, kicking up their heels and pairing off with their mothers. Not so, however, with an old billy goat, that remained in the court room thumping on the Judge's stand. He was tied hard and fast in the chair occupied by his Honor in presiding. The town gathered to see his Honor on the bench—*presiding in horns!* The boys enjoyed the result of their pranks, innocent of any knowledge as to how came the calves, and honest Billy White's old billy, in the court-room. It all passed off as a joke, intended for the ears of the Judge of the "Court of Pleas and Quarter Sessions," who was in the habit, when on the bench, of getting dry, and calling on the Sheriff:

"Mr. Sheriff, adjourn court, and let's all go and take a *horn.*"

Many amusing incidents and anecdotes were told of old Holtshouser's court. He was firmly impressed with the idea that his court could not err; he regarded himself as the *arbiter dictum* of the court and the law, as was illustrated in the case of old Johnny Giddins. The old man had absented himself from home for some cause known only to himself. He had gone in the direction of Arkansas, fatal ground to travel over in those days. His long absence had confirmed his family and friends in the belief that he had "gone to that bourne from whence no traveler returns." Application was made to Holtshouser's court to declare his estate vacant, and for an administrator to be appointed. The requisite proof of his demise was made, and the administraton of his estate regularly opened. The usual time allowed for winding up and closing the administration elapsed, and the estate was distributed among the heirs and legatees. In the course of a short time old man Giddins turned up alive, and appeared before Holtshouser's court *persona personam*, demanding that his estate be restored to him. Holtshouser heard him through, and then replied:

"Sir, your case seems a hard one, but it can't be helped now. This court has declared that you are *extinctus defunctus*—dead! It is the decision of this court now. This court can't err. Mr. Sheriff, adjourn court, and let's all go and take a horn."

My father was very little suited for a tavern-keeper. Conscious of his personal rights, and stern in maintaining them, he exercised little patience in the short-coming of others. He worried under a practical joke. A rigid old-side Presbyterian, he believed in training up the young "in the way they should go." He put his foot down upon the night amusement of the "boys about town." It but sharpened their appetites for a little fun at his expense. The new bell, put up in the belfry, was inviting for a little innocent amusement. They began their fun, to his great annoyance, by ringing the bell in the dead hour of night. The bell was never rung at night, except a few taps for the hostler, or in the event of fire. Every few nights the bell would ring. It annoyed him so that he vowed that the next night it rang he would find out, by some strategy or other, who did it, and pepper the fellow well with duck shot. The boys were delighted that the "old 'Squire," as they called him, was annoyed; it was what they played for. They went to work, upon a strategy of their own, to increase the volume of their fun, and increase if possible, the "'Squire's" annoyance. One night (the moon was shining brightly), the bell commenced ringing; my father got up and dressed himself, and put fresh priming in his gun, charged with a load of small shot. My mother endeavored to dissuade him from going out; that it was better to let the boys alone; that they would stop ringing the bell when they found that it did not vex him. He was resolved, however, to put a stop to it; then calling up the hostler, he threw his cloak around him, and went for the bell-ringers, sending the hostler up on the building to find out by the string the boys had tied to the bell, the direction they were concealed. The bell continued to ring furiously, as if the town was on fire. The hostler reaching the top of the building, discovered the fellow that was ringing, he sliped off of the roof and down to the ground as quick as he could, saying:

"*Master! master!* I found him, he's straddle the new sign aringing all his might! come quick, he could n't help seeing me when I was on top of the house; come quick, before he gets away."

My father moved round in front, and there the fellow was, sitting straddle of the sign, pulling at the string with increased jerks, the bell ringing louder than ever.

"Come down from there, you miscreant! Come down, or I will pepper you good," he said.

The fellow's arm continued to jerk the string, and the bell kept ringing.

"Stop ringing that bell—and come down from there, or I will fill you full of shot. Won't you stop ringing that bell and come down?"

The fellow straddle the sign continued to jerk the string as though he would drive the clapper through the rim of the bell. In the meantime the town people had began to gather on the public square, the man on the sign continuing to ring furiously. My father could stand it no longer. He had given the fellow fair warning, and he still continued his aggravating jerks at the bell. He raised his gun, in the act of shooting. Tom Taylor, the lawyer, put his head out from a window above and hallooed out, "Don't shoot, don't shoot, 'Squire, it will be murder—bring a ladder."

It was too late—bang went the gun.

"Let it be murder," he said, as he brought the gun down from his face. The fellow didn't flinch, but continued jerking away at the bell-string, the bell peeling away in the clear, still moonlight. My father became excitingly mad, and vowed that he would load up with buck-shot and bring him down. Just then the ladder was brought. The hostler was ordered to go up and fetch him down.

"Bring him down," said my father, "dead or alive."

"He ain't dead, sir, see him ringing as hard as he can," said the hostler, as he went up the ladder. Reaching near enough to get hold of his leg, he gave it a tremendous jerk, bringing it away from his body, and let it drop, saying:

"There's his leg, *master*, you shot it off; he's don stop ringing now."

A good many of the town people had gathered around after the firing of the gun. When the leg dropped to the ground, with the hostler's remark, "You have shot his leg off, master," a rush was made to see it. It was neither flesh, bone, nor blood. The joke had exploded. The bell-ringer was brought down—a well-shaped man of straw, minus a leg. The "sell" was complete. Many of the town people felt that they were equally "sold" with my father, who, after the excitement passed off, enjoyed the joke in his dry way. The boys were satisfied, but nobody knew who did it. The explanation but increased the interest of the "sell." It was well-planed, as the boys about Covington knew how. The strategy was a success. The new sign stood in a line with the belfry, and the old court-house, which stood in the public square, and was two stories high. The man of straw represented a well-shaped man, dressed, capped and booted. Several strong fishing lines tied together, one end tied to the bell-clapper, and the line stretched across to the upper window of the court-house, the hand of the man of straw fastened to it, gave the operator inside of the court-house perfect control. Whenever he would pull the line, it gave the appearance of having been done by the man astraddle of the sign. It being a bright moonlight night, the operator could see through the window what was going on around the signpost, so when the hostler got hold of the man of straw the joke exploded, and the operator left his place of concealment.

A tavern or hotel was more particularly a public place than now. The public felt that it had a right to say and do pretty much as it pleased, so the bills were paid. Swearing, the taking of the Lord's name in vain, was common then as now. Nothing annoyed my father more. Vulgar and profane language he abominated; profanity at his table was beyond his endurance. Passing through the dining-room one day (it was during court week) his attention was arrested by "dam that mule! dam that mule! what a h—l-fired wicked beast he must have been!" Just then my father reached the chair of the individual using the profane language. It proved to be his old friend Major Richmond, from Brownsville, who was attending court. The humorous Major had dropped his knife and fork, had his gaze fixed in the face of another guest who had taken his seat at the table opposite him, when my father, laying his hand on the Major's shoulder, inquired the cause of such language. The Major sprang to his feet upon the instant, without taking his fixed gaze from the face of the man before him, exclaimed:

"*I was only contemning the da—, the infernal, confounded, everlastingly-wicked beast—the son or daughter of a jackass, for spoiling the beauty of that gentleman's face,*" pointing at the man across the table.

"Tot, tot, tot," says my father, "Major, that is one of our most excellent and worthy citizens—his face becomes him much. Mr. Shankle, allow me to introduce to you my old friend Major Richmond!"

Shankle accepted the introduction, and he and the humorous Major joined hands across the table, the Major humorously apologizing for his mistake. The reader must know, as all who knew him will attest, that if an "ugly club" had been formed in Tipton, our friend George Shankle would have been unanimously chosen its first president.

Major Richmond and George Shankle became firm friends after that. Shankle used his influence in getting the Major employed in all the "road cases," which, in those days, encumbered the docket on "State days." An old time and highly esteemed first settler was

MAJOR JAMES SWEENEY,

a neighbor of George Shankles. The Major kept a house of entertainment on the road from Covington to Randolph. Always in a good humor, he delighted to have his friends stop with him; fond of good eating himself, none knew better how to gratify the need and appetite of his guest. Few men were better or more favorably known in the county. He was noted for his excessive laughter, his risables ever in tention; often when alone he was known to break out in a horse laugh at some humorous thought of his own. In asking or answering questions, his habit was to use language in the *relative.* His manner and language in the use of words was peculiarly his own, rarily ever failing to produce merriment and laughter. For instance, he would walk into a store when wishing to purchase a pair of children's shoes, he would inquire of the clerk or store-keeper if they had anything *relative* to little children's running about out of doors. Knowing well his manner of expressing his wants, the store-keeper would, without further question, hand out the article called for. A party of the Major's friends was passing his house one day in the month of November; the Major was hard at work in his garden digging away with a hoe. The party halting at the fence on the roadside, hallooed to the Major inquiring what he was driving at. He rose up from his laboring posture, with one of his side-shaking laughs, saying:

"I was just getting the rust off this grubbing-hoe, by way of preparing a bed *relative* to strawberries and cream next spring." Major James Sweeny is kindly remembered by the people of Tipton for his hospitality and many kind acts.

Covington was a thriving new town; stores and business multiplying, particularly the tippling shops. People drank then, as now, except they then *took it at intervals*, but now they take it as a regular, constant drink. Liquor seemed to have more effect upon the people then than now; it may be that it was stronger, or possibly their not taking it regularly, as is done now, had something to do with it. The best men then, as they do now, "imbibed," or, in the language of the "Court of Pleas and Quarter Sessions," they all took a "horn." When court was in session, and on public days, the country emptied itself of the mail population into town, and none blushed to take a drink, who felt like it. Liquor in those days seemed to make people more belligerent than now; it may have been that they feared less to fight, because of the absence of the revolver in everybody's pocket, as is not the case in the present age. Certain it is, that never a public day passed off in Covington without sundry fights; without somebody's nose smashed, eyes gouged, or heads bruised. Liquor was said to be the cause of it all. It was very seldom that any one was fatally hurt. The first killing I remember to have occurred in Covington under the head of *murder*, was by old Tackett. We all remember old Tackett; he had killed his man in North Carolina, and escaped the gallows by fleeing to Tennessee. He put a load of squirrel-shot in Deputy Sheriff Mitchell's breast. Mitchell lived several days after he was shot. Upon a *post-mortem* examination being had, it was found that five or more shot had penetrated his heart. Tackett was tried for the murder, and found guilty of murder in the first degree; his lawyers obtained a new trial for him. Upon his second trial he was found guilty of manslaughter, and sentenced to be branded in the palm of the left hand with the letters "M. S.," which was done.

Another murder case occurred not long after yet remembered by the old citizens for the novelty of the mode of arriving at a verdict. A man by the name of Gray was accused and indicted for killing his wife. Few cases excited more interest than Gray's case; he was defended by the best talent the bar afforded, and the case occupied several days; the jury received the judge's charge late at night, being well nigh tired out from their protracted sitting during the trial. Returning to the jury room it was soon found that six were for hanging and six for clearing the criminal. Finding that they could not agree upon a verdict, they sent the baliff over to the judge's room to say that they were hung—that it was not possible for them to agree upon a verdict. The judge told the baliff to go back and inform the jury that if they did not agree upon a verdict they might remain 'hung' to the end of the term. The baliff reported back the pleasure of the Judge. They went to work again to find a verdict, but couldn't; they seemed more firmly 'hung.' To remain hung for the balance of the term was trying to their worn-out patience. When it was proposed as the shortest and the only way they could 'agree,' that the best 'old sledge' player be selected from each side of the verdict, and a game of six-card seven up decide. To this proposition they 'agreed;' a member from each side was chosen, a deck of cards brought, and the game began. Gray's life was staked upon the turning of a card. The game was close, six and six, when the juror from the clearing side turned jack. They found a verdict post haste, and the baliff was sent to bring the Judge over. The Judge was prompt in getting on the bench, and ordered the Sheriff to bring in the jury. They were standing at the door of the jury room waiting. The Clerk called over their names and asked:

"Gentlemen, have you agreed upon a verdict?" The paper was handed up and read:

"We, the jury, find the defendant not guilty."

The writer is informed that the juror who "turned up jack" is yet alive to attest the truth of history.

An aggravated stabbing under the law occurred not long after the Tackett killing, at the "movers' camping ground" near town, on the Brownsville road. Rufus Garland, a most excellent good citizen, of good family and high respectability, lived some four miles northeast of Covington. Rufus would get into a *spree* once in awhile, and when in a "spree" he was permitted by all who knew him "to have his own way." His friends, and he had many, would facilitate his vein for humor and fun, rather than oppose him. To say Rufe, "you must not do this, or that," or take hold of his horse's bridle when he should want to ride him in the galleries, or through the house, was like putting your foot upon and adder's head. Quick as an arrow from its bow, he would strike; it made no difference who. He played sweetly upon the fiddle. When in one of his sprees the fiddle was his boby. He would mount his horse, with fiddle and bow in hand, and ride, as on a race, all around the square playing. His horse was trained to suit his frolics, and seemed uqually fond of it with his master. Going up flights of steps and leaping out again was one of his favorite amusements. But Rufe's sprees finally got him into trouble. Starting home one night, (he never left town, when in a spree, until after dark), several of his friends and neighbors with him; passing the movers' camp fires he reigned up his horse and vowed he would make him leap the long log fire that was burning brightly. Heading him to it he put spurs; before reaching the fire a stout young man rose to his feet and seized the bridle and checked up the horse, with an angry oath, "I'll be damned if you do." Garland was off of his horse before his friends could get to him, perforating the young man all over his chest with his little four and a half inch dirk. Garland was a small, very small man, quick as lightning and active as a cat. The effect of liquor upon him only set his brain on fire. He had stabbed the young man in a dozen or more places, many of them fatally aimed. Doctors were sent for and they pronounced him mortally wounded. Garland got on his horse and rode home, saying that he would come to town next morning. The young man was quartered in a house near by, and properly attended and nursed; his life was dispaired of from day to day for many weeks. In the meantime Garland went to jail. It was not deemed a bailable case in the event of the death of the young man, and he was kept in jail for several weeks. The jailer was a good, jolly fellow, and having perfect confidence in Garland's integrity, he gave him the freedom of the limits of the building. The jail had just been finished; large and new. The jailer with his family lived in it. He was a tinner by trade, and had his shop in one of the rooms of the jail. Garland had him to make a tin fiddle, which he strung up and amused himself with making tinny music. The people from the country, as well as town, flocked to the jail to see the tin fiddle and hear Rufus play on it. The reader can well imagine the character of sound that would come from a tin fiddle. It was artistically made in all its parts, with sound-post, and well strung. With the magic bow in Rufus' hand it in very truth gave out sweet strains of tinny music. Those who were boys then can certainly never forget Rufus Garland's tin fiddle.

The young man finally got well; Garland was bailed out, and what the verdict of the jury was in the case is not within the recollection of the writer, there being no malice in the case, and Garland being a worthy good citizen of property and standing, it fell among the ordinary cases of assault and battery.

THE HIGH AND WELL-MERITED CHARACTER OF THE LATE GRANDVILLE D. SEARCY

is deserving more than a brief sketch, and a far better historic pen than mine. A long and strong personal attachment which existed between the writer and the subject of this brief notice, beginning when he entered upon his career in Covington, running through a quarter of a century, renders the duty, however, a pleasing one. His high and well-merited character as a man and a lawyer ranked him pre-emintly among the men of mark in West Tennessee. In manners, easy and graceful, soul full of warm, generous impulses. His personel was attractive and captivating upon sight. His countenance, unvarying in its reflex of kind and generous sentiment, was the admiration of every person; unclouded intelligence scintilated from every feature. A mind comprehensive with purity of thought, intuitively correct, fertile in expedient and imaginery, few were better fitted for the profession of the law. Clearness and simplicity marked his forensic efforts before both court and jury. When most vehement, and, not unfrequently, when the occasion was great, his full, clear, ringing voice rose to the climax of eloquence itself. As a lawyer or advocate, he avoided the arts and *crooked ways* known as "*sharp practice*," ever maintaining the dignity and purity of the profession. He was fitted for every station at the bar, and no lawyer was more successful in his cases. Before a jury, his manner was earnest and most impressive, never trying their patience; seizing upon the strong points in the case, he held their minds enchanted, until, as by intuition, he read in their faces a verdict. As a criminal lawyer he had no superior—he was the lion at the bar on "State days."

An incident occurred in one of his efforts before the jury at Covington court, illustrative of his great self-possession and capacity of turning to his advantage an incident calculated to break a link in the argument or confuse the case. It was a case in which the character of his client was attempted to be aspersed by the breath of slander; the argument against him had been strong and ingenious. At the moment when Colonel Searcy had reached the *acme* of his best forensic effort; when his genial face was beaming with expressions irresistible; his rich, full voice thrilling in interest and delight to the intelligent peers of the land, by an excited justiculation the stove behind him was jostled, and down fell the long stove pipe upon the floor, between the speaker and the jury box, separating at every joint and filling the court room and jurors full of dust and soot. Simultaneously with the rising of the dust and soot a gust of wind came through the windows (it was a blustering March day) dissipating the dust and soot, greatly to the relief of the jury. The incident, instead of interrupting or clowding the brilliant and glowing eloquence of the speaker, it rose higher and brighter. Seizing upon the mishap as opportune, and *tipical* of the *downfall* and breaking assunder of the ingenious argument of his adversary, he pointed to the stove pipe on the floor which had fallen apart; from which came the dust and soot like the foul breath of slander, with which it was attempted to *blacken* and asperse the character and fair name of his client, and which was dispelled and dissipated by the refreshing breeze; wafted away by the pure breath of heaven. His manner was majestic, and his eloquence burning and electric—it gave him the verdict. It is mentioned that the jury, in recurring to the case and the incident many years after, spoke of it as their "*stove-pipe verdict.*"

With no other source of income but that arising from his large and lucrative practice to support a large family, he was kept from engaging in other fields of intellectual combat, save on incidental occassions. Possessing in a high degree the mind and attributes, happily fitting him for the statesman, his name was often mentioned in connection with the United States Senate. He had made a distinguishing mark as a political debator. In accord with the great statesmen Clay and Webster in political sentiment, the complexion of the rule in popular politics was adverse to him. Colonel Searcy was a native of Tennessee, his father was for many years Clerk of the Federal Court at Nashville, where he read law. Admitted to the bar in early life, he began his career in the practice at Covington upon the organizing of the first courts of that county. He removed to Somerville in 1840, and soon afterward fixed his residence in Memphis, where he died in 1854, in the fullness of his well-merited honors, and in the vigor of his usefulness. As a friend and companion, his geniality of soul and temper linked him to his fellow-man as with "hooks of steel."

THE FOURTH OF JULY AT COVINGTON, AND COLONEL CROCKETT.

Colonel Crockett felt that his valuable services in the Twentieth Congress in behalf of his immediate constituents and the republic at large, entitled him to a re-election. His advent in the Congress of the United States had given rise to many interesting anecdotes, and amusing incidents and caricatures. The representative of the Big Hatchie District had lost nothing of his popularity; on the contrary it had rather increased by the aid of "Jack Downing" and other wits and humorous writers of the period. The Colonel entered the canvass of 1829, with a bold and confident front. He had worked in the anti-administration party, afterwards called the Jackson party. He was anti-tariff in favor of economic reform, and letting the *actual set-*

8

tler have his land at a "bit an acre." The Colonel was not permitted, however, to run through the canvass alone; opponents came out thick and strong; the field was a large one, embracing all of *thirteen* counties—Madison, Haywood, Henderson, McNary, Hardeman, Fayette, Shelby, Tipton, Gibson, Carroll, Weakly, Henry and Perry. Colonel Adam R. Alexander, of Shelby, felt that his merit and capacity was equal to the duties devolving upon a Congressman. Captain Joel Estes, a worthy and highly respectable citizen, north of Big Hatchie in Haywood, was a candidate. The Captain was among the earliest emigrant settlers in the Big Hatchie country, a native of "the Mother of Presidents" in old times, and, withall, a gentleman of more than ordinary ability. He sought to reach the hearts and minds of the voters of the district by addressing them through a lengthy circular, instead of taking the field and stump. James H. Clarke, of Tipton, a merchant and rising man of Covington, who had worked himself up from a peddler's wagon to a brick store, enterprising and ambitious, his mind was turned in the direction of Washington, and he became a candidate against Colonel Crockett. Politics began to run high, an the *mileage* was no inconsiderable object.

On the Fourth of July of that year Colonel Crockett and several of his opponents met at Covington. The "glorious Fourth" was a big day in 'old times,' without being made more glorious by the presence of such distinguished personages. It was the spread-eagle day in the land, and everybody and his neighbor was there, and for a wonder it neither thundered or rained.

Before noontide, the curling blue smoke through the dark green foliage of the tall elm, and the still taller oak, was seen ascending from the long barbecuing pits on the hill to the southwest of town, indicating the place for the people to gather at. It was in the grove where protracted revival meetings were usually held. A large bush arbor had been made, and a broad platform stand erected for the orator and distinguished persons to occupy. Yankee White was the orator of the day—Yankee was prefixed to his name to distinguish him from the other Whites of the town, beside, he came from Yankee-land, and was a very good citizen; he came within a few votes, on one occasion, of being elected to the Legislature. The day was propitious; the bright sunshine made everything look gay and beautiful, and all present were patriotically happy. Several volunteer companies were on hand handsomely uniformed. The order of the day was announced from the court-house door. The procession formed on the public square and moved toward the grove, animated by the fife and the drum, discoursing national music. As the procession neared the stand erected for the "occasion," the horses and mules hitched to the young saplings and swinging limbs of the trees became inspirited, and began prancing and dancing around their moorings. Getting still nearer, many became excited, broke lose and vaulted away through the moving masses, with saddle-skirts flapping. Midst the neighing and snorts of the animated and excited horses, whickering of colts and braying of mules; with the drum and fife, and the sea of the moving masses of men, women and children, closing in for position and place, and the clear, blue smoke passing up through the long rows of pigs, shoats, lambs, mutton and veal, smoking and brown, with fumes most appetising, the *glorious Fourth* was marshalled in. The stand was filled with the men of the day, and, after the reading of the *Declaration of Independence*: "We hold these truths to be self-evident, that all men are born equal," etc., after the order of old times celebration, the orator of the day rose and delivered his "Spread Eagle" speech to the sea of upturned faces, whose souls, filled with patriotic impulses, made more glorious the "occasion" by repeated shouts and clapping of hands. Then came the dinner—the barbecue—spread out, on long tables covered with clean, white linen. The well browned and juicy ribs and saddles, bread baskets piled up with home-made risen bread of both corn and flour, pots and pans of rich chicken pie, interspersed with tarts, pies, puddings, cakes and pickles for the girls (appetizing even to write about), enough for all, and basketsful to carry home.

Dinner over, and toasts through with, a call was made for the candidates for Congress to take the stand. Crockett! Crockett! from an hundred voices. The Colonel ascended the stand, took off his hat, deliberately pulled off his coat, and hung it up, presenting himself in his shirtsleeves, midst deafening applause and huzzahs. The evening was close and hot—not a breeze stirring, save from the numerous turkey-tail fans in motion, in the hands of the patriotic matrons present. The recollection of the writer does not serve him in giving even a synopsis of the Colonel's speech. It was plain and sensible, however, with now and then a dry, witty allusion to his educated opponents, which would bring down thunders of applause and "*hurray for Crockett*," and "*hurray for Davy.*" "Be sure you are right, then go ahead." The Colonel was followed by the other candidates in order, the last speaker being Major Jim Clarke. Excusing himself on account of the lateness of the hour, he simply announced himself a candidate for a seat in the Congress of the United States; saying that it was getting late in the afternoon. That, for a wonder, it had not rained on the "glorious Fourth;" that, judging others by himself, he concluded that "all were getting dry. That over at his store were five five-gallon demijohns, which would speak for him in the fullness of the spirit with which they were filled." With such a talk, the Major leaped from the stand, and shouted for all to follow him. Clarke had made a "ten-strike," leaving no dead wood behind him. It was the only one he made in the canvass. The day of the election was close at hand. The result of the vote was, for Crockett, 6,786; Alexander, 4,300; Estes, 132, and Clarke 9. Clarke, it is due his memory, as well as the history of the canvass, to say withdrew from the field, and engaged in the building of a turnpike across the Big Hatchie bottom, where his hard earning went drifting with the turbulent waters of the river.

In justice to the memory of Captain Joel Estes, who was perhaps the most intellectual of the candidates in the field, it may not be inappropriate as a part of the history of the times, to allow a place in these pages, for the following, taken from the Jackson *Gazette*, a newspaper then published in Jackson, Madison county, by Colonel D. C. McLean. It appeared in the issue of that paper of the 15th of August, 1829. The election having been held on the first Monday of the same month.

[For the Gazette

"Mr. Editor: As the election is now over, perhaps it would not be amiss, nay, justice, to say what was the cause of Captain Estes not holding a better poll. A great excitement having been raised among the people by the friends of the two great political champions of the West, Colonels Crockett and Alexander, that a correct, mild and independent political course was swallowed up in the vortex of ambitious buzzing. It is to be hoped that the time is not far distant when this electioneering mania will cease, and true merit, untrameled by party spirit, will assume her dignity of character.

[Signed] "A Voter."

As a specimen of the amusing interest the representative of thirteen counties in West Tennessee afforded to the newspaper men of those days, I copy entire a speech the Colonel is reported to have made during the canvass of 1829, by a correspondent of the *Missouri Republican*. The correspondent writes thus:

"The honorable Mr. Crockett, being on the day of election at one of the hustings in Tennessee, and having heard two of his able opponents address the people, was at a loss how to attract their attention to the remarks he wished to make, and asked the gentleman who had just spoken how he should effect his object, to which the gentleman replied (intending to quiz), 'mount that stump and cry, a bear to be skined.' Davy taking it litterally, mounted the stump, and sung out at the top of his voice, 'A bear to be skinned,' when the crowd gathered around him, and he began:

"'FRIENDS, FELLOW-CITIZENS, BROTHERS AND SISTERS: On the first Tuesday, previous to next Saturday, you will be called on to perform one of the most important duties that belong to free white folks—that are a fact. On that day you will be called upon to elect your members to the Senate and House of Representatives in the Congress of the United States, and feeling that in times of great political commotion like these, it becomes you to be well represented, I feel no hesitation in offering myself as a candidate to represent such a high-minded and magnanimous white set.

"'Friends, fellow-citizens, brothers and sisters: Carroll is a statesman, Jackson is a hero, and Crockett is a *horse!!*

"'Friends, fellow-citizens, brothers and sisters: They accuse me of adultery, it's a lie—I never ran away with any man's wife, that was not willing, in my life. They accuse me of gambling, it's a lie—for I always plank down the cash.

" 'Friends, fellow-citizens, brothers and sisters: They accuse me of being a drunkard, it's a d--d eternal lie—for whisky can't make me drunk.' "

CAPTER VIII.

The Mountain Academy—James. Holmes, D. D., His Pupils—My Room-Mate—Style of Dress—Camp-Meeting —Youth and Love.

NORTH of the Big Hatchie was yet a part of Tipton. It was not until 1836–7 that it was embraced in the county of Lauderdale, which was established in that year.

My father had become satisfied with his experiment at tavern-keeping, and returned to the old homestead north of the Hatchie. As yet there were no good schools in Tipton north of the Hatchie. My next eldest brother, who was being educated for a lawyer, was sent to college at Nashville, and I to the "Mountain Academy," an institution just founded by the Reverend James Holmes.

The establishing of the "Mountain Academy" marked an era in the educational department of Tipton, and no one contributed more to the forming of a correct state of the society of the county than its able and accomplished founder and principal. The school was long noted as the best in West Tennessee, and hundreds of youths were instruced and trained there, who became eminent as teachers and professional men. The name of James Holmes, D. D., is more intimately connected with West

Tennessee as an educator and instructor of the young, both male and female, than, perhaps, any other man of letters. Imbued with the fundamental principles of practical philosophy, his every undertaking was marked by the clearest light of reason and sound jundgment. As a man, he lived a life of Christain virtues, ignorant of remorse, and blameless.

Mr. Holmes was a native of Pennsylvania, his birth-place Carlye. His father died when he was in his childhood, leaving him to the tender care and training of a pious mother. He was noted in early life for his studious habits; graduating at Dickinson College before he was twenty-one, he repaired to Prinston, and entered the theological school. His feeble state of health, however, required that he should relax his studies for the ministery, and seek a recuperating field; none better offered than the mission among the Chickasaw Indians, which he accepted in his twenty-third year.

In 1824, we find him among the Chickasaws, opening a school for the teaching and training of the red children of the forest. The reader can picture to himself the youthful missionary assembling the red men of the wilderness, grouped under the shadows of the noble forest trees, near where Pontotoc, Mississippi, now stands. The old chief and his braves, seated upon the ground, the old men, women and children, forming the back ground of the picture, with the young graduate standing erect before them, relating the object of his mission.

Alone in that wild territory he stood, in the spring time of life, away from old associates and familiar scenes. May we not conclude that his language and words spoken, were in the spirit of the great and pure founder of his native State. When speaking to the Algonquins he said:

"We meet on the broad pathway of good faith and good will. I will not call you children nor brothers only, for brothers differ. The friendship between you and me, I will not compare to a chain, for that the rains might rust or a fallen tree break. We are the same as if one man's body were to be divided in two parts. We are all one flesh and one blood"—(pointing to the heaven above)

'Where the souls of *heathens* go,
Wh) better live than we, though less they know.'"

Mr. Holmes labored among the Chickasaws from 1824 to 1833, when it was decided to remove them west of the Mississippi.

As a mark of the high esteem in which he was held by the Chiakasaws, a large number of Indian girls and boys followed him to Tipton, and remained under his tutilage until they were required to return to join their red friends in their removal West.

The second year of Mr. Holmes' sojourn among the Chickasaws he was accepted as the husband of the noble and heroic Miss Sarah Van Wagenon, of Newark, N. J., whose first wedding tour was among the children of the forest, who cheerfully exchanged the luxuries and comforts, the pleasures and enjoyments of the cultivated and refined society of her native city, and braved the perils and hardships incident to life in a savage territory, to live with the man she loved, and share with him his pleasures and triumphs. Few wives are marked with such heroism. Mrs. Homes survives her noble husband, after a happy wedded life of forty-seven years.

The "Mountain Church" was organized in his house in 1834, and he was made a ruling elder. Feeble lungs, and consequent weak voice, debared him from taking an active part in the ministry. In the early history of the "Mountain Church" an occasion offered illustrative of his great character and influence. It is related that some difficulty grew up in the church, difficult to settle, and likely to work harm. When the cloud of discord portended evil, and was most thrilling, his smooth, even-tempered good sense lighted up the reason of the contentious, producing an immediate, amicable adjustment. He possessed in a high degree a sagacity of mind which enabled him to separate that which belongs to individual prejudice from that which commends itself to the more *rational.* He ever avoided the jars and jarring of men, and controversies. His words, at all times "freighted with truth," commanded the ear and enjoyed the confidence of all men.

The degree of D. D. was conferred on him in 1846. In 1849 he was elected to the Presidency of the West Tennessee College at Jackson. The college never prospered more than while under his management. Still preserving his love and attachment for the people of Tipton, with fond memories of his early teaching at the "Mountain," he dissolved his connection with the college at Jackson, and fixed his residence in Covington, taking charge of the "Female Seminary" at that place, which continued under his management up to the time of his death. That large band of young women, who live to adorn the society of West Tennessee, trace with pride and pleasure their training and education and refined deportment back to the "Mountain Academy" and the "Female Seminary," and attest the truth of this brief sketch of my old preceptor, whose memory we alike venerate.

I had commenced this brief sketch of Mr. Holmes, and had written to him asking a synopsis of his early life, and was answered by his son, referring me to an obituary notice of him.

A more loving character I never knew—a theme worthy a better pen. His long and eventful life has become history; his noble Christian virtues live embalmed in the memories of all who knew him. He had lived all the days allotted to man; born on the 21st of August, 1801, and died on the — day of February, 1873, in the seventy-first year of his age.

A touching incident, beautifully illustrative of the wonderful power and influence exercised by Mr. Holmes over those who fell under his training and pupilage, I may be permitted to relate a story told me, most interesting in Indian life. On the fourth Chickasaw bluff, in the vicinity where Court Square is situated, long before Memphis was a village, at the mouth of Wolf, stood an Indian hut, the dwelling place of a half-breed; (his wife was a full blood). From them sprang many sons. One of them, the eldest, perhaps, mingled much with the whites as they came in and settled upon the bluff. He soon learned to drink whisky, and like most whisky drinkers, became dissolute. Wishing likewise to acquire a knowledge of books, to read and write like the white man, he resolved to join the school of instruction, which had commenced its operation by Mr. H. Holmes. Prevailing on others of his associates to go with him, it was soon arranged and the day fixed for them to start. Filling his pack and binding up his blanket, none were found ready on the day appointed but himself. In his eagerness, he left alone and on foot to join the missionary school, situated near where Pontotoc now stands. At noontide he stopped by the side of a bright running stream for rest, and to refresh himself from his scanty stores. Seated on the bank of the stream, its bright waters rippling at his feet, alone in the deep shades of his native forest, he drew from his pack, among other things, a bottle of whisky. Holding it up in the clear sunlight he began to reflect—as he had never done before—of the evil and trouble whisky had brought upon his race. Casting his eye down upon the clear rippling waters flowing beneath his feet, without uncorking his bottle he returned it to his pack, refreshed himself from the waters of the branch, ate of his scanty supplies, and resumed his tramp toward the missionary school. When night overtook him he rolled himself up in his blanket and slept alone in the wilderness. Refreshed by sleep, he rose early, and resumed his earnest steps, until he reached a suitable place for rest and eating. Taking out his bottle of whisky again he withdrew the stopper. When in the act of putting the fiery fluid to his lips, the same thoughts rushed upon him again. Rising to his feet, and without tasting, he dashed it against the nearest tree. Refreshing himself again from the bright waters of the wilderness, he ate his frugal meal and continued his walk. Reaching the missionary station—it was on the Sabbath—his people had already gathered at the chappel in the shady grove, he made his way to it and took his seat among them. He had learned to speak and understand English, and was an attentive listener to the man of God. In the discriptive portion of the discourse, as it fell from the lips of the pure Christian man, truthful to nature and most touching and gentle in its delineation of human devices aimed for the destruction of man, the young red man realized his own situation, and read in the strong picture of human misery and sin, drawn to very life, the picture of himself. Illustrating most truthfully incidents and scenes connected with his past career, he concluded at once that the story of his past life had been told to the preacher. Rising to his feet in the midst of the discourse, he slowly glanced his eyes over the gathered multitude to see if some of his companions and associates were not there; whether they had not arrived ahead of him and related to the good missionary much of the truth of what he was saying. Finding none of the those his eyes had searched for, he rusumed his seat riviting his eyes upon the divine speaker. It seemed to him that the burden of the discourse was specially directed at him. He rose again and scaned the members present. Finding none that he knew among his bluff associates, he sank upon his seat. The spirit of the white man's God had revealed to him the whole truth and he became a Christian.

I boarded with "the best man in the world," old Father Wilson. The Reverend Hugh Wilson was a co-laborer with Mr. Holmes, as a missionary and teacher among the Chickasaws; his aim and object in teaching at the "Mountain" was to establish a "Manual Laboring School," the experiment failed, however, and he migrated to Texas.

My room-mate was a rising young man—a benneficiary scholar—under the auspices of the Presbytery sent to the "Mountain," to be educated for the ministry. A pure, pious Christian was Andrew Allison, also a beneficiary, and boarded with father Wilson. Everybody loved Allison, and nobody loved my room-mate, yet he loved himself—the very embodiment of selfishness. Born so, he couldn't help it; ugly as home-made sin, yet he was vain enough to think himself handsome; that he was vain in that, I will put his picture in a frame, and the reader can judge.

In hight, he was under the average of men in that day, he might have been five feet five, with more body than legs, very square in the shoulders, with arms, when standing erect, reaching to the tops of his boot-legs, hands broader than a beaver's tail, with fingers like young "handspikes." Darwin would have selected him as a fair specimen of the "Origin of Man." His hair black and shiney, kept so by the profuse use of bears-greese; eyes small and likewise black, glistening like a chinquepin; dark skin, thick and bumpy, with mouth and nose not unlike other people. Yet, his mouth had its expression more peculiar to himself than other people, lips rather thin, were long enough to lap over, but he had a way of sucking them in at the corners, as if they had been stained with molasses. But his foot, he wore a No. 11 brogan, being rights and lefts, the right shoe was a better fit on the left foot, as was the left shoe a better fit on the right foot. To wear them thus, the toes of his shoes didn't turn out any. He was rather inclined to be bow-legged and slightly pigeon-toed. Such is my recollection of the person of my friend and room-mate, while at the "Mountain Academy." He was *sanctimoniously pious.* Not much in sympathy with him, I was often the subject of a pious lecture from him. He rather took it upon himself to keep me in the "strait way," especially on Sabbath days. An incident occurred while we were pupils together, and dwelling in the same log-cabin, that gave me the mastery over him, and put an end to his pious lectures, greatly to my relief. Father Wilson and his good wife, with whom we boarded, were of the old "blue stocking" order. Nothing was allowed to be cooked on the Sabbath. *Cold corn risen bread* I abominated, besides two meals were rather short, even in the short days of early fall. The potato patch being convenient, I made out, without grumbling. My room-mate, like myself, was fond of roasted potatoes. The patch was very convenient. We had to pass through it in getting to the cabin we occupied, and he was an expert grabbler. He had a quick eye in discovering the best hills. Circling his long, "hand-spike" fingers around a well-filled hill, he would bring out a mess at a haul. On Sundays, however, he would neither grabble or eat, and lectured me for the "sin of the thing." I took his lectures for what they were worth, roasting rather more on Sunday nights, to make up for the loss of my third meal:

It was the habit of my room-mate to spend his Sabbath evenings down at the house with Father Wilson and the family, seldom returing to the cabin until after prayers. One Sunday night I filled the fire full of potatoes, and walked up the hill to pay a visit to my eldest sister, who was likewise a pupil of Mr. Holmes, and boarded with him. My visit was necessarily cut short, to return and look after my potatoes. When nearing the cabin, I discovered some one through the cracks of the logs stiring in the fire. I quickened my pace, reaching the door, I shoved it wide open, and who should it be but my pious room-mate, from whom I expected a moral lecture for violating the Sabbath day. He had taken out one of my best yams, (having smoothed the ashes over the remaining ones), and was in the act of blowing the ashes off of it as I stepped in.

"Halloo!" says I, "you here? Is prayers over?" He had began to squirm and twist himself around in the chair. Replying to me, he whined out (it was his habit to droll out his words), and said that he was "feeling bad—that he had a sorter *griping*." His discomforture was so great, that I began to feel for him, and rattle away some nonsense or other. In the meantime he was squirming as though in pain, while shoving my yam down into his breeches pocket. It soon began to burn beyond his endurance, when he rose, and made a quick move for the door, the steam rising from the smoking-hot yam, as he made his exit. I called to him to "hold on, I would go to prayers with him." Pulling my potatoes out on the hearth, I leaped out of the door, and followed him, keeping so close that he could make no disposition of his hot tormentor. It was terrible on him. Tight pants were then the style. He had on his best Sundays. The tights kept his burning companion close up to his skin. On he went leaning to it, until we reached the house, and opening the door, we found the family making preparation for prayers. We sank down in the nearest chairs, when Father Wilson called on Allison to read. During the reading, my room-mate was very restless, twisting about in his seat, attracting the attention of Mother Wilson. My frame of mind was greatly in sympathy with his suffering—wondering whether he could get *his frame* of mind in the straight way by the time the reading was through with, as he surely would be called on to pray. The sacred book closed; we all went down upon our knees, and he was called on to pray. I never before heard him pray so well; he prayed hard and earnest for all sinful flesh—for us not to be *tempted*; that we should not *hunger* after that which was forbidden, dwelling long upon the *total depravity* of man. As he warmed up the potatoes cooled down. I had forgiven him—he had merited forgiveness, and I freely forgave him in that, that I never let him know that I had caught him in an *ashey trick.* The joke was too good to be kept from Allison.

The first camp-meeting held in that part of the country was in the course of preparation, in the Clopton settlement, some six miles from the "Mountain." I may be permitted to make myself the hero, in showing off the fashion and style of dress, as well as a ridiculous *mishap*, forming an incident in real life.

It was seldom that I missed going to a big meeting or a ball, when in reach of me. To this camp-meeting I was bound to go. It came to my knowledge that a party from Randolph would be there, with whom a certain young lady would surely come, which greatly increased my anxiety to go. It was about the time for me to get a new suit of clothes. To get them made, and in time for the camp-meeting I went into Covington two weeks before hand, and ordered them, resolving to be in the *tip and hight* of the fashion. I went to Bill McGaughey, a fashionable young tailor. Bill had just received his fall fashions—the latest styles from New York and Philadelphia. He was a very fine artist in the way of getting up a good fit. I was well shaped for eighteen—stood six feet in silk stockings and dancing pumps. Only lacking in flesh, Bill and myself were the same size to a button. He always wore fine fitting clothes of his own make, illustrative of the style, as well as the art he had attained in his trade. He took my measure for coat, vest and pants. The cloth for the suit, with full trimmings, buckrum and buttons, with black silk velvet for the collar, was sent to his shop. The cloth for the coat, brown; style, frock; coming down to the knees; vest, buff casimere, with bright gilt buttons; and pants, pongee silk, lavender color.

The handsome young professor of the "goose" and I were good friends. He promised me a good fit, and in time for the camp-meeting. I returned to the "Mountain," well pleased with myself and the rest of mankind.

The time having elapsed for my suit to be ready, I went in for it. They were ready, and I tried them on. The fit was charming. Bill had added another leaf to his laurels for being the best-fitting tailor in town.

The coat set well upon my square shoulders; the tail full, and coming well down to the knees, with its high double-breasted rolling collar. The pants were in the tip of the style—tights—fitting tight as the skin from the knees up—increasing in looseness down to the foot; buttoned down with broad straps. The vest of a light buff cassimere, with fancy gilt buttons—buttoned up to the throat. I felt that none would be at the camp-meeting better dressed or more in the style, and was all axiety to be on the ground. My friend Bill put them up in a neat parcel, and I returned to the "Mountain." I was up the next morning bright and early. I had procured a horse from Elder Lynn, and borrowed Father Wilson's saddle.

The riding on horse back six or more miles in my pongees troubled me, lest they should become soiled. I had wrapped the stirrup-leathers and lengthened them out, to keep from bending my knees, as much as possible. In *prim trim* I was ready to mount. The horse was a tall one. Finding it difficult to bend the knee, I sought a stump, vaulted into the saddle and road away at a rapid pace, to keep ahead of the crowd. An hour's ride brought me in sight of the smoke and bustle of the camp-grounds. The site had been well selected in the heart of the forest; the undergrowth grubbed out, the young trees trimmed up, and avenues opened. Every possible attention had been given to render the grounds pleasant and inviting. It seemed as though everybody was there. For hundreds of yards around the stand every available bush and hitching place had been appropriated.

Riding around to find a safe place for hitching, and a convenient log or stump to aid me in dismounting, I came upon the carriages and vehicles of the Randolph party. By accident I had fallen into the company of friends and acquaintances. My horse was taken in charge, and an invitation to make the carriages my headquarters. I was not long in finding out that Miss C. was of the party. My feelings were ixexpressible—in a maze of delight at my good luck. Either I was in love, or I was not; I felt that I was. And if I was not, it was all the same as if it were a veritable fact. I had met her before, and not always "by chance." The last time we met was at a ball, and we danced together more than once, and twice in succession; and, wearied not of each other. It had not taken a serious shape, however. I had only played upon the surface. Yet I was within a stride of deep water. I soon learned that the field was not alone to me; a rival was upon the ground in close attendance. He was a dangerous one; for he was rich, beside he had wit, and was most agreeable. But he was old in years—double my age; yet he was good looking and tall; only a little ball on the top of his head, with flowing black locks. He looked best with his hat on.

I felt my youth, and never was more proud of it. I was vain enough to think it would eventuate to my advantage. I feared only his riches. She, like myself, was young and ardent. It was most natural for young people to love one another. We soon met; he joked me about her, and complimented my tailor. I was pleased and flattered. I became bold, and felt like "taking the bull by the horns." I *was* in love. The ladies of the party were up at the stand. We walked leisurely to join them. They were grouped together on the outskirts of the stand. A glancing look told me that her eyes were upon us. Casting my eyes down upon my pongees, and adjusting my coat collar, I left my old bachelor friend and rival, and moved with the elasticity of vain youth and joined the party. She was the belle and center of attraction in the little circle. Young, blithe and fresh, gay and frolicsome as a sportive lamb of a May morning, tall and most bewitchingly shaped, with clusters of bright, gloosy light-brown hair falling around her broad white forehead, long lashes, a shade darker, fringing over the purest blue eye, large and clear, reflecting a generous, loving nature—the very soul of love. Voice rich, full and musical as it fell from her choral lips; with her silvery laugh she was perfectly irresistible. Every feature of her young, loving face in unison with a soul born to love, scintillated a pleasurable hope, as I walked up and clasped her soft, ungloved hand with a warm and impressive shake, a gleam of affectionate pleasure lighted up her countenance, assuring me that our greeting was agreeable—that she yet remembered when last we danced together.

It was yet an hour before the noon service would begin. I suggested a stroll in the grove, offering my arm (quite a fashion in those days). Taking it, she expressed her delight that the opportunity offered by which she could escape the gaze of so many new faces. Passing near my old batchelor friend and rival, who yet remained where I had left him, and who had been a "looker-on," a furtive glance came from under his dark brows. We passed on in a sportive manner and talk, regardless of the consequent remarks of the lookers-on, or the curious inquisitive, until we reached the carriages of the party. Entering the one she had came up in, we were alone to ourselves. Counting not the joyous, happy moments (hours were as but moments to us), we were alone until the hour for noon service to begin, in a delirium of delight and love—joyous as a loving dream, until the spell was broken by voices nearing the carriage. Several ladies and gentlemen of the party, including my rival, came up. To relieve the situation, which, by their approach, had become a little embarrassing and to show off the agility of youth I made a spring, leaping a dozen or more feet, lighting in a hard place, turning my ankle; my knees gave way, and in the effort to recover my feet my pongees gave way—*bursted* from knees to hip; naught saving my utter exposure but the long-tail brown. My chagrin was inexpressible. Making the best of an hour's love and triumph, I slept with my room-mate that night.

CHAPTER IX.

Randolph in Old Times—Its Better Days—Lost the Chance of Becoming a City—Spirit of Internal Improvement of that Day—Early Settlers—First Newspaper in the County—The Murrell Excitement—Expedition to Shawne Villagee.

RANDOLPH, at the period it is the purpose of this chapter to introduce to the reader, was the most flourishing business river town in West Tennessee, on the Mississippi. It was the "receiving and forwarding" town for Tipton, Haywood, Fayette, Madison, and Hardeman. Eligibly situated immediately below the mouth of the Big Hatchie, which was navigable for small steamboats as high up as Bolivar, it received a considerable trade from the counties east of Madison and Hardeman.

Had the project of connecting the waters of the Tennessee river with the Hatchie, as was suggested by a few enterprising men of that day, and recommended by Governor Cannon in his annual message to the Legislature, been carried into effect, the whole trade and trafic of North Alabama and the Tennessee valley would have fallen into the lap of Randolph, and Memphis would have remained a "village at the mouth of Wolf" for an indefinite number of years. The age of progress, however, was yet in the womb of time. The political prejudice of the day was, for the most part, averse to projects of internal improvement. For the life and trade of Randolph, it happened to be in the infant days of Democracy, when the minds of the people were being educated in the doctrine of "strict construction." The Southern bias was taking root, Jackson, Clay, Crawford and Adams giving shape to new parties founded upon the economic management of the government. Mr. Monroe, then President, had elaborated the subject of the power of Congress to grant aid and foster works of internal improvement, and took grounds against it. The few enterprising men in the Big Hatchie country had their appetites sharpened by the success and popularity of the subject along the northern lakes, where canals were being cut. The great Clinton, of the State of New York, had taken the "bull by the horns," and practically demonstrated the utility and advantage of such public work. With like feelings and enlarged views, they regarded the example a a good one, and sought to apply it to the development of their own section. It was no go, however. The strict-construction and economic party thought nature ought to take its course. They thought it best to permit the Tennessee river to continue to roll on in her *transverse* course, washing the shores of a higher latitude, and entering the Mississippi, with the waters of the Ohio, two hundred miles above the mouth of the Big Hatchie.

As a specimen of the narrow views to which the people were being trained and educated in those days, in reference to works of a public character, the proposition for the construction of a post-road from opposite Memphis to Little Rock, amply illustrates, and is referred to as a part of the history of "Old Times."

Among the many communications to the press of that period, I copy the following from the Jackson *Gazette*, a newspaper published in Jackson in 1826. It purports to be from the pen of one of the leading men of that day. It begins thus:

"MR. PRINTER—In looking over the last week's *Gazette*, I notice, with *astonishment* and *surprise*, that Congress has ordered a road to be cut, at *public* expense, from the *Village of Memphis*, better known as the Chickasaw Bluffs, on the Mississippi river, to Little Rock, in Arkansas territory. The making of this new proposed road will cost the United States an *immense sum of money*, and little or no good will result from it except it will be to *hold out the idea* that Memphis, like the famed city after which it is named, is conspicious upon the general plan of the map of our State—an Indian trading post, at most, insulated from Tennessee. The minds of the people have become *heated* and *intoxicated* upon the subject of *internal improvement.* This *mania* for internal improvement, I fear, will never rest until it has caused the United States Treasury to be *disgorged* of her last shilling. There are, in my opinion, such things as national sins, and though punishment to individuals may be reserved to another world, national punishment can only be inflicted in this. The evils we are suffering must be put an end to."

Now, reader, what think you was the amount appropriated by Congress, out of the United States Treasury, toward cutting the proposed road? To be exact, it was eleven thousand six hundred and seventy-four dollars and eighteen and three quarter cents. So Randolph, after holding Memphis in check for fifteen or more years, lost her only chance of becoming a city—the largest commercial city in West Tennessee.

The removal of the Chickasaw Indians west of the Mississippi river, and consequent bringing into cultivation the rich and fertile lands of North Mississippi, facilitated the birth of the era of railroads to Memphis, and Randolph waned. As Memphis prospered Randolph declined, until her merchants and business men drifted with the current of prosperity, and landed at the mouth of Wolf. Bayless, Bowles, Smithers, Stewart, Laurence, Steel, Booker, Temple, Latham, and many others, who did business under the bluff at Randolph, changed the heading of their ledgers, and posted in their earnings from the bluff at Memphis. Randolph as it was, is now only in name, and lives alone in the history of "Old Times in the Big Hatchie Country."

The rich and fertile table lands in the vicinity of Randolph early attracted men of wealth and intelligence. Among the first was

JESSEE BENTON,

who settled below Randolph, on the Mississippi, before 1824, as in that year we find him a candidate on the Presidential electoral ticket as a Crawford elector. Memphis was the nearest postoffice. Implacable, with singularly strong personal prejudice, he became a law unto himself, and soon migrated, when menaced by settled neighborhoods, to a more frontier country—Texas. Uncompromising in his personal predilections and opinions, it is said that he was inexorable in his enmity toward his brother Thomas H., and General Jackson. Many incidents illustrative of his character are remembered, the following, possibly, the strongest: He had entrusted a lot of stock to an individual in whom he had confidence, to take to Louisiana and sell. Upon his return, he reported that he had been robbed on his way back, of the money. Benton rejected his story, and required that he produce the money or suffer such torture as he thought fit to inflict upon him. He still vowed that he had been robbed. The implacable Benton did not, or feigned not to believe, and ordered his overseer, with several negro men, to take him across the river to an island and box him up in a certain hollow tree, and there to be kept, without food and water, until he disgorged or told the truth about the money. They did as he commanded—dared not do otherwise. After several days he went over to receive his confession, making the negroes take a cross-cut saw along. The hollow tree afforded just room enough for his victim to stand upright. In that position he had been kept more than three days. Finding that he could not starve him out (for he still held to his same story), he ordered a couple of negro fellows to take hold of the saw and saw the tree down. To work they went, the saw soon cutting its way into the hollow.

The delinquent, finding it was Benton's intention not only to saw the tree down but to saw him into, cried out, as soon as the sharp teeth began to menace his flesh, to hold on, that he would tell all the truth. With a most pitiable wail for his life, he told that he had gone into a gambling house in New Orleans and lost all his own money, and in trying to get it back he had staked up Benton's money, and lost that, and had to work his passage back, etc. Benton, believing that he had gotten the whole truth out of the fellow, spared his life. In the meantime courts had been organized in the county, and the matter got before the grand jury.

Orvil Shelby, a generous, kind-hearted, genial companion and neighbor, became the owner of, and fixed his place of residence upon, the "Benton place," and contributed to the interest and advancement of society in and around Randolph. The

ALSTONS,

in whose veins coursed the best blood of the "Old North State," established a large plantation several miles back, and became, by their native courtesy and good manners, an acquisition to the society of the village and vicinity. They owned two of the best fiddlers the followers of Terpsichore ever danced after—Jim and Ossian—father and son. They were the pupils of the celebrated North Carolina violinist, Iley Nunn. They played at all the balls in the county, and were often sent for to play at Jackson and Brownsville.

Colonel Tom Robertson lived a happy life "up on the hill," the "latch-string" of whose door was always on the outside. Generous and most hospitable, full of anecdote and passionately fond of a good joke, he entertained gloriously. One good laugh of his would dispel the *ennui* of the village.

FRANK LATHAM

was the pioneer newspaper man of Tipton. He early settled at Randolph, and published the Randolph *Recorder*, a "rich, rare and spicey" little sheet, whose editor was most excellent good company. Noted for his lively, personal character, with a genial smile always upon his ruddy face, without blemish in the "social," he was a welcome guest in every household. Life with Frank Latham, in "old times," was ever in the merry sunshine. He yet enjoys life in the shade of venerable years.

Randolph came in for her share of the Murrell excitement, prevalent in those days. The "Murrell Clan" were not myths; they were veritable men of extraordinary boldness and daring. They counted their numbers by hundreds, and ranged from the Walnut Hills, at the mouth of the Yazoo, to the mouth of the Big Hatchie. They held their "Grand Council" in the deep, dark woods of the Mississippi bottom, in Aakansas, twelve or more miles below Randolph and some six miles from the river, near Shawnee Village. The writer yet retains a lively recollection of the many scenes and incidents of that thrilling and eventful period. Robbery, theft and murder occupied and filled the minds and engaged the attention of the people from Vicksburg to New Madrid. It was the theme in the quiet family circle, as well as public talk, and the subject of municipal ordinances and regulations. Every town along the river had its vigilant committee and patrol, for the protection of life and property. Randolph had its vigilant committee and organized patrol, and every stranger that entered the town and neighborhood was "spotted" until his business and personal became satisfactorily known to the guardians of the town.

The Clansmen's most usual place of crossing the Mississippi, was a short distance below the "Benton place." In tracking their way to and from the "Grand Council Tree," a notable sycamore, standing in the tickest of the deep forest, towering above all other trees—discernible for miles around—a beacon to guide the foot-steps of the Clan in gathering. They seldom traveled over the same trail more than once, that they might elude the vigil of all who were not of their clan. The size of the "Council Tree," at its base, equaled the notable Indiana sycamore at the mouth of the Big Pigeon, which is said to measure, at its base, seventy-five feet around, and capable of stabling in its capacious hollow, twenty-four horses at a time. It was at this tree, and in its great hollow, that John A. Murrell and his Clansmen met in grand council, and formed their dark plots, and concocted their hellish plans. Most of their depredations were committed along the river, and in the night time. Seldom a night passed at Randolph without the capture of *suspicious persons.* It is keenly remembered by the writer, who was a member of the patrol at Randolph, in those "dark and bloody days," that one dark night (the darker the night the better for their wicked purposes, and the greater the necessity for the patrol to be on the alert), the patrol were out on the river front above town. In the dead, silent hours of the night, the gentle rippling of the still waters from the sharp prow of a boat came gliding down near the shore. The patrol had taken a position at the mouth of a deep cove, formed by the flow of the waters from the high bluff. It afforded a safe mooring for small boats. The suspicious craft moved in close to shore, and ran into the cove. Several yards from the river's edge, waiting until they had made fast by running an oar down in the soft mud, when the Captain of the patrol threw the light from his dark lantern full upon them, the patrol at the same time leveling their double barrels. Three stout, broad-shouldered sinners stood before us; an old gray-haired lark, and two younger—father and his two sons. The old man, who stood in the stern of the boat, dropped something from his shoulder into the water as soon as discovered. The water being shallow, however, he was required to fish it up. It proved to be a wallet filled with burglar's tools. They were marched up to the headquarters of the vigilance committee, and immediately put upon trial under the code of Judge Lynch. The wallet contained sufficient evidence to insure conviction and speedy execution. On account of the gray hairs of the old sinner, and youth of his two sons, the penalty was modified to corporeal castigation. They were sentenced to be denuded of every vestige of their clothes, stretched across a cotton bale, and striped with a three and a half foot "cowhide," at intervals, until day began to break, the old man to receive two licks to the boys one. That when day began to dawn, that they be taken to their boat, stark naked, tied hand and foot, and fast to the bottom of the boat, face upwards, gagged, with a placard posted upon their foreheads, written upon each, that if "ever caught again on the east bank of the Mississippi, in Tennessee, a twenty-five pound bag of shot would be tied around their necks and they become food for the catfish;" the boat to be carriedout in the middle of the current and sent adrift without oars. The sentence was fully executed, and their up-turned faces greeted the first rays of the morning sun.

It was during those bloody days that an occurrence happened some twelve miles below Randolph that shocked the whole country. A most atrocious and diabolical wholesale murder and robbery had been committed on the Arkansas side. The crew of a flatboat had been murdered in cold blood, disemboweled and thrown in the river, and the boat-stores appropriated among the perpetrators of the foul deed. The "Murrell Clan" were charged with the inhuman and devilish act. Public meetings were called in different parts of the country to devise means to rid the country and clear the woods of the "Clan," and to bring to immediate punishment the murderers of the flatboatmen. In Covington a company was formed to that end, under the command of Maj. Hockley and Grandville D. Searcy, and one, also, formed in Randolph, under the command of Colonel Orvil Shelby. They met at Randolph and organized into one company, under command of Colonel Shelby. A flatboat, suited to the purpose, was procured, and the expedition, consisting of some eighty or an hundred men, well armed, with several days' rations, floated out from Randolph, and down to the landing where the wholesale murder had been committed. Their place of destination was Shawnee Village, some six or moie miles from the Mississippi, where the Sheriff of the county resided. They were first to require of the Sheriff to put the offenders under arrest, and turn them over to be dealt with according to law. To Shawnee Village the expedition moved in single file, along a tortuous trail through the thick cane and jungle, until within a few miles of the village, when the whole line was startled by a shrill whistle at the head of the column, answered by the sharp click! click! click! of the cocking of the rifles in the hands of the Clansmen, in ambush, to the right flank of the moving file, and within less than a dozen yards.

The chief of the Clan stepped out at the head of the expedition, and in a *stentorian voice* commanded the expedition to halt! saying:

"We have man for man; move forward another step and a rifle bullet will be sent through every man under your command."

A parley was had, when more than man for man of the Clansmen rose from their hiding places in the thick cane, with their guns at a present. The expedition had fallen into a trap; the Clansmen had not been idle in finding out the movements against them across the river. Doubtless many of them had been in attendance at the meetings held for the purpose of their destruction. The movement had been a rash one, and nothing was left to be done but to adopt the axiom that "prudence is the better part of valor." The leaders of the expedition were permitted to communicate with the Sheriff, who *promised* to do what he could in having the offenders brought to justice; but, alas for Arkansas and justice! the Sheriff himself was thought to be in sympathy with the Clan, and the law was in the hands of the Clansmen. The expedition retraced their steps. Had it not been so formidable, and well known by the Clansmen, every member of it would have found his grave in the Arkansas swamp.

It was not long after, when, through the heroism of Virgil A. Stewart, John A. Murrell fell into his trap, which resulted in the Clan being scattered, and their organization broken up.

CHAPTER X.

Lauderdale Formed out of Big Hatchie Territory—Key Corner Established by Henry Rutherford, in 1789—Rutherford and Porter the First Permanent Settlers—David T. Porter the First Born—Cole Creek Bluffs—Interesting Topographical Features—Discovery of the Three Graves; Their History Worked out in Romance.

TIPTON, north of Hatchie, together with a slip off the northwestern corner of Haywood, and a fair loaf off of the southwestern part of Dyer, formed the present limits of Lauderdale, which was erected into a county by an act of the Legislature in the year 1835.

The first magistrates appointed for the county were Robert C. Campbell, Benjamin F. Johnson, Jeremiah Patrick, Milton G. Turner, John H. Maxwell, Able H. Pope, William Strain, Elijah B. Foster, Henry Critchfield, Cristopher G. Litsworth, Henry R. Crawford and Henry R. Chambers. They met at the house of Samuel Lusk the following year (1836), and organized the first County Court, electing Robert C. Campbell, Chairman; William Carigan, Clerk; Guy Smith, Sheriff; Isaac Bradon, Coroner; Samuel Lusk, Ranger; Thomas Fisher, Register; William T. Morehead, Trustee; Milton G. Turner, John H. Maxwell, Able H. Pope and Robert W. Campbell, Revenue Commissioners;

Griffeth L. Rutherford, R. S. Byrn, Hiram C. Keller, Henry R. Crawford and Robert W. Campbell, Commissioners to sell the lots in the newly established county town, Ripley.

The first Circuit Court was held at the house of George Byler, in 1836, and David Gilliland appointed the first Clerk. It is not within the limits of the plan fixed by the writer of these reminiscences to treat of the period when Lauderdale became an independent county. The territory forming the county, being within the limits of the Big Hatchie country in "old times," takes in "Key Corner" and the "Cole Creek Bluffs," which is not more interesting for its wild and romantic scenery, than bordering the famed hunting ground of Davy Crockett, and the many incidents in pioneer life.

KEY CORNER

dates its history from the year 1789. When the State of North Carolina meditated the transfer of her territorial rights to the lands embraced within the limits of the present State of Tennessee to Congress, with a view of its being erected into a State, certain owners of North Carolina land grants obtained the services of Henry Rutherford, a surveyor, to push forward west of the Tennessee river, upon the lands then owned by the Chickasaws, and make certain locations. Rutherford, organizing his surveying party on the Cumberland, descended that river in the fall of the year 1789. Working their way down to the mouth of the Forked Deer, he poled up that stream until he struck the first high land, which happened to be at the point of intersection of the Cole Creek Bluffs with the Forked Deer river. There he landed, and made his first mark upon a small sycamore tree in the shape of a key, which he established as the corner of his future surveys, from which time (1789) it has been known as the "Key Corner" upon all the maps of subsequent surveys.

In 1819–20, Henry Rutherford and David Porter found their way down the Cumberland and up the Forked Deer, and made a permanent settlement at the "Key Corner," which became the nucleus of the first settlement on the Forked Deer river, which, before the counties of Tipton, Haywood and Dyer were formed, was known as the "Key Corner Settlement." Henry Rutherford and David Porter were among the first prominent settlers in West Tennessee, and among the most pominent men. The first "grist mill" was built at "Key Corner," known as "Rutherford's Mill." The first settlers about Brownsville sent their corn to the "Key Corner" to be ground. Rutherford was made County Surveyor, which office he filled as long as he lived, preserving to the day of his death, which occurred but a few years ago, remarkable good health, and a most wonderful recollection of the early incidents of his life, and marked with clearness and precision the surveys made by him more than three score of years back.

The first child born on the territory embraced within the limits of Lauderdale county, was

DAVID T. PORTER,

in the year 1820, at the "Key Corner." Reared in

the house of his birth, he is honored by having never lived anywhere else. Like the fixedness and stability of Rutherford's sycamore, he has lived fifty-three years at the same place, having, during that time, resided in three counties by continuing to live at home. Prominent among his neighbors, and highly esteemed for his courage and manly bearing, he was made a Captain in the Confederate service, which position he filled with honor.

John Flippin came from Knox county and settled near the "Key Corner" in the year 1822, and shared with the early pioneers the perils and hardships of the wilderness, and left his name identified with the land of his early adoption through his sons; the most prominent of whom, Benjamin M. Flippin, is yet living in Lauderdale in the vicinity where his father first settled.

The Cole Creek Bluffs, beginning at the "Key Corner," on the Forked Deer, range southwest to the upper point of the first Chickasaw Bluff, on the Mississippi river, a distance of some fifteen or more miles, and constitute the most interesting topographical features of Lauderdale county. They overlook that large body of bottom land lying to the west and north—the land of the many newly-made lakes—the famed hunting-ground in "old times," when the screw-cutter and Davy Crockett hunted together, before the rents and cracks produced by the shakes of 1811–12 had all healed over.

It was on the highest knob of this range of bluffs, within near distance of the great Father of Waters, the god of day, which had been intensely bright, was fast losing its force upon the hills, its glancing rays diffusing a gentle fading crimson through the yellow-tinted foliage of the wild-woods, reflecting back a bright golden luster from the tops of the far off trees to the east; looking to the far west, over the tops of the ocean of tall trees that shaded the broad acres below, the eye no longer contracted by the "sharp sunbeam," the full vision gazed upon one uniform glory. The lakes had received into their placid bosom the last lingering ray of the sunset. 'Way yonder, across the mighty river, the flitting fragment of a cloud, with its purple edges, lingers, the fading luster of the crimson blending until the shades of night gain possession of the heavens. How good it was in "our Father in Heaven" to give us the "moon and stars to shine by night;" how cheerless and gloomy the world would have been without them—the very thought of black darkness makes one shudder. Gloom and ghostly apparitions seize hold of his very thoughts. The moon and stars never shone brighter, however, than they did that night on the screw-cutter and his little hunter companion. By accident they had pitched upon the loveliest spot on the bluffs, far above the gloom of the dark shades of the deep woods below them; through the tops of the tall trees the eye penetrated and caught glimpses of the bright waters of the lakes trembling in the silvery luster 'neath the full moon in mid-heaven. Upon that lovely knoll they yielded to "tired nature" their first night upon the Cole Creek Bluffs, in the early part of the month of November, 182—. Rolled up in their blankets, they sought the "sweet restorer, balmy sleep."

Neither cloud nor displeasure marred the glory of the morning. The gray streaks of the early morn gave promise of a fair day. Taking their morning meal—tender steaks cut from the loin of a yearling deer the screw-cutter had shot down the evening before—they wandered away to find a spring of fresh water. Winding down the high hill, they struck a bright little stream of running water, and followed the course of its curving up a deep gorge. Soon the gorge narrowed, barely allowing room to pass between the branch and the high overhanging bluff sides. Going through the narrow pass, they stepped into a lovely little glen of several rods in width—a most enchanting little spot, the margin of the bright little branch grown over with tall water-lilies, embowered by the thick overhanging foliage from the steep hill-sides, terminating at the head by a perpendicular bluff, from under which gushed a bold spring.

"See! see there! it's an old, abandoned hut in a state of decay. Yes, it is the remains of an old mud hut, the front and one end crushed in by the shivering of that stately oak; 'twas a thunder-bolt that did it. Well, if this isn't a discovery in this wild, uninhabited country. Halloo! the world is coming to an end, surely. No, those who once inhabited this quiet little nook found their end; for, as I am alive, they are dead. Here is three well-marked graves. One of them seems old—old of long standing; the other two seemingly of more recent date, yet quite old enough for their friends, if they have any, to forget them; it is so odd. Oh! that the dead could speak from their long and lonely resting place; what a tale, perhaps of sorrow and tears, could be told here."

"Sit down under the shadows of this grove of elm and oak by the side of that gurgling spring of bright water, and after thou wilt have refreshed thyself, let the imagination work it out.

"Many years ago I had a young and fast friend. We were in the habit of hunting these woods—hunting down the Obion to its mouth, and up Reelfoot, spending months in the chase together," said the screw-cutter. "Young, handsome and brave-hearted, I loved him dearly. The sight of those graves revives in me a sad remembrance; they bring to mind what I had well nigh forgotten. Sad memories! Could the living reunite the dry bones beneath those little hillocks and clothe them in the freshness of youth, what a tale of romance could be told of these woods. Enough is remembered, however, to remove the mystery that hangs over them.

"On the occasion of our last hunt in these woods we had been out several weeks. My hunting companion became strangely afflicted for a hunter. After our morning meal, he would take his gun and be gone all day, returning to the camp after nightfall happy and gay, without reporting the killing of any game. In answer to inquiries as to his day's hunt, he would express himself the happiest man in the world, giving a most glowing description of a beautiful lake he had discovered some three or four hours' walk from the camp.

"A more noble fellow or braver hunter never shouldered a rifle. He became a maniac. Those graves must have had something to do with his going crazy. The lake we got a glimpse of last night is doubtless the same he was so fond of talking about.

"The story is a long one, I will tell it as we go along. We must go back to our horses now."

They started back to their horses, continuing the narrative as they went along.

"My hunting companion returned to camp one night more thoughtful than usual, expressing himself tired of the hunt, and urged that we break up camp. We had killed more bear than we could well pack away; beside, the hunt, from the turn of mind my young friend had taken, had pretty much lost its interest. We ended the hunt and returned to the settlement. We separated. He returned to his home. He lived with an aged mother near the Madrid settlement.

"When the next hunting season came round he did not join us. It was a year after before we met again. Wild and uncontrollable, he had abandoned himself to the wild haunts in the woods. It was in the woods that we met. He threw his arms around me, embracing me with the fond affection of a brother, shedding tears as a child. The scenes when last we had been together seemed to haunt him. The burden of his wild talk was of the beautiful lake and his lovely 'White Lily.' I carried him home to his old mother. He neither ate nor slept. I remained with him until he died.

"After his death his old mother took from an old secretary a roll of papers. Handing them to me, she said:

"'Victor's last request, before he lost his mind, was that after his death I should hand these papers to you; that they would unravel a mystery.'

"Thus the story runs:

"'Curious to examine the sunk lakes, lower down from where our camp was pitched, I had walked several hours in a southern direction, when I came upon a beautiful open lake, the loveliest I had discovered in the bottom. I struck the head of it, from which point I obtained a full view of its length and size. Tray-shaped, it was longer than it was broad—perhaps three or more miles long. Like most lakes, it was shallow around the margin, getting deeper in the middle; judging from its being open in the middle, and other appearances, deeper than the tallest of surrounding forest trees. It being free from undergrowth and fallen timbers along the margin, I strolled around it. In passing along, my attention was attracted by the fish darting from near the shore into deep water. The lake seemed to be alive with them.

"'Coming to a shady spot, where a large tree had blown up, falling over the lake, its strong roots holding it suspended over the surface of the water, I halted to rest. Setting my gun by the roots, I walked out on it several feet from the shore and lay down upon its huge trunk. My attention was soon attracted to a clump of tall water-lilies growing in the water near the shore, by the jumping and floundering of the fish; so charmed with the countless numbers of the finny tribe darting through the clear sunny spots upon the bright surface of the water, passing to and fro among the lilies, that I must have been there an hour or more when the sound of a gentle rippling of the waters, rapidly approaching from behind me, arrested my attention. Without rising from my reclining position, I turned my head and eyes full upon the loveliest form in human flesh I ever beheld—a young woman standing erect in a trim little canoe, driving its sharp prow swiftly over the surface of the placid water. So great was my amazement that I felt transfixed to the log. Her long golden hair thrown back upon her shoulders, her head uncapped; fair as a lily, and fresh as a new-born rose, she was a very picture of female beauty and loveliness just budding into womanhood. Looking neither to the right nor left, her eyes fixed upon the clump of water lilies, she gently raised her long slender paddle out of the water, the sharp bow of her little boat gliding in among them. She had not observed me, so intently were her eyes peering down into the clear water. Schools of the bright scaly tribe closed in around her, flouncing and cutting up all sorts of finny antics. Running her long paddle down in the soft mud to steady her little boat, intent alone upon the object of her mission, she stooped forward, her long golden locks falling over her face. She seated herself in the bottom of her frail little craft, burying her head among the tall lilies, humming in a soft musical strain, as in converse with the countless numbers of fish that gathered around her. There she remained, feeding and chanting to her little lake companions, within a rod of me.

"'My eyes, from gazing so intently upon such a dazzling beauty, began to grow blind. I expected every moment that the loud beating of my heart would arrest her attention. In such a delirium of delight and amazement, I felt pinned fast to the tree. The opportunity, however, was favorable for rising from my recumbent position. In an instant I was upon my feet, as yet wholly unobserved by the fair queen of the lake.

"'Getting through with her little charities and talk with her finny companions, now and then running her long white hand under the clear water, the little silvery-sided tribe gathering around it, and passing through her long tapering fingers, bidding them good-bye for the evening, she arose to her feet, and we stood face to face. The excited amazement which had held me spell-bound, had began to pass off. It came her time to exhibit surprise and amazement. Throwing her large, clear, blue eyes full upon me, raising both of her hands, throwing back her long, yellow tresses, she imploringly said: 'Who! and what are you! and why are you here?'

"'Her manner was bewitchingly earnest. In words as gentle and soothing as possible, I replied:

"'I am a hunter, and came in these woods to hunt; that in rambling about in the woods, I came upon this lake, and was attracted to this enchanting spot, where I have been for hours, amusing myself with the movements of the numerous beautiful fish passing to and fro among the tall lilies.' Having replied to her two pointed questions, I then asked her to tell me who she was, and why she was alone upon this beautiful lake in the wild-woods?'

"'Who I am, I beg you will not inquire, or seek to know. I am here to feed and commune with my little lake companions, where I have not failed to be since my childhood. I beg that you will ask me no more questions, or seek to find me out, and that you will not again come to this lake,' her voice softening and becoming more subdued as she finished speaking, still keeping her large blue eyes in a fixed gaze upon me.

"'I begged that she would not lay upon me such a burden, or to seal my lips against nature's ardent promptings. That I would have to be more than human to abide her biddings. That it was asking more than the human heart could stand.

"'In what have I put upon you more than is human to bear?' she said, her voice still softening.

"'Why, in requiring that I shall not seek to know you, or find you out, now that I have seen you; that we have met and spoken, that I know these woods contain one so beautiful and lovely, the thing you ask is impossible.'

"'Then you will destroy all the pleasures I have in life. I can come to these enchanting waters no more. I will never see and commune with my little lake companions any more,' said she, a soft, sorrowing gloom suffusing her sweet face as she pronounced the last words.

"'I then asked her to answer me a few more questions; whether she had parents, or whether she was alone in the wild forest.

"'Mother I have not; I know nothing of a mother. I have an old father who is good to me; I love and honor him above all things except my Bible. I have promised him, and he exacts the promise to be renewed every year, that I will decline the acquaintance of all persons; that the time will come, and soon enough, when I will know of the world and a new life, but not until after his death.'

"'Have you ever met with any one in these woods before?' I inquired.

"'Never; you are the first and only man I ever saw, save my old father. From him I have learned much. I have read much of the world. I read from my Bible that the world is full of sin, and man is desperately wicked.' All the while she had not taken her eyes from me. She seemed charmed by the first specimen of young flesh in human form. With softened tone of expression she seemed willing to prolong the interview.

"'I said to her that the wild-woods was my home, my companions were my dogs and my gun, young and full of warm impulses; that in her limited knowledge of the world, as derived from books, she knew but little of the human heart. That she, like myself, had a heart full of generous, loving impulses; that from the Bible she had read that man and woman were made for each other, and to make one another happy, and that it was not good to be 'alone in the world.'

"'Yes, the Bible reads that way. We read of the first man and the first woman in the garden. We read that they were happy until a knowledge of the world brought sin.'

"'Imploringly I asked that I might talk with her when she came again to hold converse with her lake companions. I promised that I would then abide whatever her decision might be. Before she had spoken, I read in her melting blue eyes her answer. She replied, 'I promise.' With the word ringing in my ears, she shoved her little bark out in the deep water and shot across the lake. I stood gazing upon her receding form until it was lost to view in the thick foliage overhanging the margin of the lake on the opposite shore.

"'The next day I was at the lake long before the hour of her coming. I lingered around the enchanting spot of our meeting the previous day. Prompt in coming, I kept out of her view until she should have gotten through with her pleasing, self-imposed duties. I could but observe that when approaching the lilies, she raised those large blue eyes and took in a survey on land. I was greatly encouraged to hope. After she had gotten through with the scaly tribe (she seemed more hurried than on the evening before), she rose to her feet, when I discovered myself to her. She came upon shore, extending her hand. We strolled down the lake shore in the silent wood. We talked of a new life, and whispered love to each other. Upon the silent shores of the 'Lake of the Lilies' we plighted our love, with a 'promise' that I should visit her old father at his secluded dwelling-place the next day.

"'At the appointed hour the next day we met on the opposite shore of the lake. A short walk through the dark forest brought us to a deep ravine winding up in the hills, through which flowed a bright little rippling brook. Reaching the head of it the banks became bluff, deeply shaded over by the thick foliage of the giant forest overhead. From under the bluff gushed a bold spring. The old trapper hermit was seated before the door of his mud hut. As we approached he rose to his feet with the dignity and true politeness of an old time gentleman, his long silvery locks falling down over his broad shoulders, with snow white beard covering his well-formed chest. He extended his hand to me, saying:

"'The White Lily, my daughter, the light of my life, has told me all. It is only that which I most feared, and possibly had a right to expect. Her young life knows nothing of sorrow or disappointment; mastering all the studies and knowledge I was able to teach or capable of imparting, yet she is ignorant of the world and a stranger to sin.

"'For fifteen years she has been the light and life of an old man, who lives a trespasser upon many years beyond the period allotted to man upon earth. It is not surprising that her ardent young nature, loving as it is, should have accepted the heart and hand of young flesh, one like yourself, who seem the gentleman, though a hunter. I am only a trapper; I have faith that you are a true man, and will make her a good husband. My age forbids that I should oppose her wishes; I fear to risk doing her an injustice; I have been to her a good guardian and father.'

"'Taking her hand and putting it in mine, he bade us to kneel before him. Laying a hand upon each of our heads he said:

"'Receive the blessing of the old trapper Nichol. Two months and four days from to-day will be my ninety-fourth birthday. On that day, which will be my last, I will take the White Lily, the light and life of my last day, to the settlement at Madrid; be there, and she becomes your wife. Until then, upon the pain of your losing her, come not to this place again.'

"'So long! two months and four days; permit me to come for her,' says I.

"'No! you are the only person who has visited this place or seen me in these woods, or the White Lily since I first saw yon spring, now more than fifty-seven years ago, save him whose remains lie 'neath that moss-covered grave at the end of this cabin and the young woman who shall be your prize for keeping away. Let it be so.'

"'With his last words, 'shall be *your prize* for keeping away,' I turned to join her at the spring, and the old trapper disappeared in his dark hut. Our last hour upon the green velvet moss by the side of the rippling brook was as a love dream—a delirium of blissful delight.

"'Two months and four days—sixty-four days to

wait! Had it been a sentence to the scaffold, time would have been craved; but—well, I have to wait. The two months came round; but the four days and four long nights—each day seemed a month, and the last of the four I thought would never pass. It seemed as though the sun would never reach noontide; that, as in the days of Joshua, it had been bidden to stand still.

"'The two months and four days had passed. I stood upon the bluff at the place appointed for me to receive the object of love—the sole absorbing object of my heart's affection. With lengthened vision my eyes kept watch to get the first glimpse of the old trapper, with the 'light of his life,' as they should hove in sight below. Hour after hour I stood, and not an object came in sight upon the broad waters of the great river. With straining eyes I stood alone upon the bank looking down the reach, until with heavy heart I turned my face from the waters, when the eye could no longer penetrate through the darkness of the night. On the bank I walked—walked all night, with ear sharpened to catch the sound of the oars' stroke. None came, and broad daylight found me with eyes still open peering down the river. In the agony of my soul I stepped into the first boat and pushed off to meet them. Down I rowed, on I pulled; never did skiff glide over water faster. Glancing at every turn back over my shoulder to get a sight of their coming, I relaxed not a stroke of the oar until night came upon me.

"'Reaching the point of landing the nearest to

the old trapper's hut as the morning sun rose over the high point of the first Chickasaw Bluff, I bounded away for the 'Lake of the Lilies.' I easily found my way to the old trapper's hut. Casting from me the gloomy spell which had bound me for the past twenty-four hours, doubting not that ought else than the whim and caprice of an old man who felt that he was parting with the light and life of his last days detained her, I moved up the sparkling branch with new life.

"'Reaching the hut, the door was closed. Signs of life had departed in every direction the eye turned. There was no smoke curling up from the broad throat of the cabin—gloom and desolation seized hold of my senses. With dread awe, I stood at the door of the hut, with hand raised to rap, when my eyes fell upon a newly-made grave by the side of the ancient moss-covered one. Overwhelmed with a presentiment of woe, I leaned heavily against the door, when it swung open, upon its heavy grating hinges, exposing to view the lifeless form of the old Trapper. Dead, dead, dead! Half alive I lay upon the door step. A voice from 'neath the fresh clod ringing through my ears, dead, dead, dead! Staggering, I arose, and strode to the spring, the still voice following—tingling in my ears, penetrating to the soul, dead, dead, dead! More dead than alive, I fell upon the green moss, where last we had talked and dreamed in a wild delirium of bliss and happiness. 'Twas here she had grown up, and enjoyed the early fruits of her young life—here, under the shades of the overhanging foliage, now drooping in silent sorrow, shedding their virgin tears upon her newly-made grave. Up yonder hill-side, she frisked and frolicked, with the young morning, blythe and gay as a young May lamb. Oh! life, even in spring time, thou art but 'a poor pensioner upon the bounties of an hour.' For hours I lay as in a dream, living life over again. It all seemed wrapped up in a few days of the near past; fortune I had none; the light and promise of the future had gone; vacancy, broad sterile vacancy, loomed up before me. It had taken the place of all that was lovely. I had aught now to live for. Near me the gurgling waters arose from beneath the high bluff, playing with the bright sunbeam as they rippled past in their silvery, winding course down the gorge. I arose, and bathed my feverish temples in the cool refreshing waters, and went to the cabin, to put away the old Trapper, in remembrance of her, and because she loved and honored him. He lay as though he had died under a Christian hand; every limb in its proper place, his head resting upon a roll of rare furs, his hands clasped across his broad chest, in one a small slip of paper, upon which was written: 'Bury my body by the side of the newly-made grave, where sleeps the light of my life—April 4, —.' Signed Nichol. The light of his life had gone before him. He died on his ninety-fourth birthday—the day of his appointment.

"'Near him, on a rude table, lay a roll of manuscript. On the outer side was written: 'For the affianced of the 'White Lily.' Here, then, is the mistery. Oh! manhood, why hast thou forsaken me? I was once called when in the chase, 'Victor, the lion-hearted.' I am no longer the 'lion-hearted.' The soft illurements of woman's love has won the victory—the grave has become the victor, and left its sting—the barbed arrow corroding in my bleeding soul. But the mistery. We will read it after putting the old man away.

FROM NICHOLS' MANUSCRIPT.

"On the fourth day of April, should I be living, I will have lived to see my ninety-fourth birthday, and for more than fifty-seven years I have lived a trapper hermit, in this hut.

"On my twenty-sixth birthday I married with a lovely English woman, the daughter of a British officer, stationed on Lake Erie. She was fair and rosey, gentle in disposition, and free from guile. My love for her knew no bounds. We had been married four years, when I carried her and our only child, a daughter, our darling little Marie, to stay with her father at Fort Pitt, until my return from a fur-hunting expedition on the upper lakes. I had expected to be gone but one winter. Fortune did not favor us, however, and we were absent two years. During that time the war-whoop was raised on the lakes—the Pontiac war broke out, of which we had heard nothing, until on our way back, at Green Bay. I had a presentiment, foreboding evil to my wife and child, and neither ate or slept until I reached the fort. Too truly had been my fears and misgivings. Both wife and child were butchered and scalped by the ruthless savage.

"I remembered nothing more from the day of my arrival in the fort until some four months after, when I found myself under the treatment of the kind physician of the fort. When I was sufficiently recovered to be permitted to leave the fort, I met with a warm friend and companion. We had messed together and slept under the same blanket during our two winters on the upper lakes. He knew of my deep affliction and sympathized with me, advising that I leave the scenes of the lake and go south to Louisiana. I agreed—would have agreed to have gone with him anywhere, as for myself I cared not which way it was. We soon were ready with a good boat and requisite outfit for the trip. Reaching the Mississippi we soon passed the mouth of the Ohio. It was in the month of August, the weather very hot, and the water bad to drink. My friend took sick and was getting worse every day. Reaching the first high bluff after many days drifting, we stopped to find good water, and a cool, shady place, intending to remain until cool weather before proceeding on down the river. After many hours' search I found this spring of delightful water in this cool, shady nook in the woods. Returning to the boat, my friend being just able to walk out to it, I went to work and packed out our traps and things. He drank heartily of the cool water that evening and felt greatly refreshed. In the morning he felt much better. Before noon, however, he was taken with a chill and died in it. I buried him where he died, and built this hut by the side of his grave, resolved never to leave it while life lasted. Here I have lived, and alone during the first forty odd years, occasionally taking a trip up the river to dispose of my furs and lay in needed supplies. I trapped it up the Obion, indeed up all the water courses, and through the bottom for thirty miles up the river. At home in the woods, I only returned to my hut when my wallet became exhausted.

"I witnessed many of the wonderful freaks of nature in those awful days of earthquakes and shakes. During the worst of it I had gone up the Obion, roaming through the bottom in search of beaver *sign*. My attention was arrested by a rumbling noise. At first I thought it the approach of a storm or big wind. Soon the sound seemed to be everywhere, and from the bowels of the earth it became fearful. I tried to gather in my thoughts and fix in my mind what to look for. When the ground upon which I stood began to tremble, heave and shake with terrific violence, the vibrations becoming quicker and more terrible, until it became impossible to stand upon my feet without holding on to the small trees around me. I knew not which way to turn or whither to go for safety. The giant forest around and over me swayed and groaned, clashing and crashing their great laps, keeping time with the undulating movement of the earth in which they were rooted. Soon the earth began to quake, and crack around and beneath where I was standing. In the wildest confusion it began to break and open before me, then to sink, sink, sink, carrying down with it a great park of trees, until the tops of the tallest among them dropped out of sight. In awe and wonderment I stood reeling as one drunk with wine, and witnessed the birth of Reelfoot Lake.

"My boat! I had left it in a nook, near the Obion. Fearing to lose it, I made for it in quick haste. The waters had ebbed from it, leaving it high and dry. Soon, however, the flow returned, with the violence of a mountain torrent. Lashing it to a small tree, I succeeded in keeping it from being 'swamped.' The waters becoming sufficiently quiet, I rowed down the mouth, passing out with the flow of the waters, which had filled the whole bottom many feet. In passing up the gorge, to my hut, I found that my spring branch had gone dry. On reaching the spring, the first thing noticeable was a fearful rent in the bluff, reaching down below the spring-bed, and not a drop of water in it. 'Confusion worse confounded' seemed spread out all over the land. Openings appeared as by magic from the high hills to the great Father of Waters, many newly-formed lakes had been created in close proximity to my heretofore seemingly safe and quiet dwelling-place. The loss of my spring! I had begun to thirst, and water was not to be had nearer than the newly-made lakes. I had begun to think of the necessity of finding a new place of abode, when the earth began to tremble and quake again, the air soon becoming suffused with a sulphuerous smell. I sat in my cabin and waited the terrible pending results, when I noticed the hurried flow of black muddy water leaping down the spring branch, sweeping and bending the herbage and small undergrowth in its angry surging course. Having lost all personal fear midst the terrible freaks of the earth and water around me, I arose, and walked to the spring, to witness the changes going on. The deep split in the bluff had closed up as though under the power of a great battering-ram. Black muddy water was gushing up through the spring and all around it, emitting a most disagreeable odor. Soon the flow of water began to decrease and get clear; before night-fall my spring had resumed its ancient *regime.*

"The next morning I had gone to the river to look after my boat; while standing upon the bank, I noticed a boat drifting in the current. Rowing out to it, I was amazed beyond fitting language to express, to find lying in the bottom of the drifting skiff a lovely child, her sweeet little face turned up to the heavens. At first I could not tell whether she was living or dead. Her long brown lashes were fringed over her closed eyes; her bright golden curls had fallen back, exposing to the sharp rays of the sun the most angelic-like face I had ever beheld. I stood looking upon her lovely features as in a dream, when an angelic smile came to her sweet countenance, followed by a soft and gentle breathing. She was not dead—only sleeping.

"Gently I fastened the drifting craft to mine and pulled for the shore. My boat coming up to the bank abruptly, jarring the boat she was in, startled her. In a moment I was in the boat with her, taking a seat to steady it as she arose to her little feet, rubbing her eyes, seemingly not yet fully awake. Opening her large clear blue eyes, she discovered me. Springing into my arms, she cried out:

"'Oh! papa, papa; where is mamma?'

"Burying her sweet little face in my bosom for several moments, I pressed her little head to my heart, stroking her soft hair, while scalding tears came trickling down over my old brown, furrowed cheeks. Her angelic face had struck a cord in my heart, calling up before me my murdered wife and child. I held in my bosom the *image* of my long lost little Marie, and pressed her little face to my aching heart.

"She raised her little head, looking me full in the face, and fixing her clear blue eyes on mine, she spoke, saying:

"'I thought you was papa. I don't know *you.* What makes you cry?'

"Moments passed before I could give utterance to a word. Recovering myself, however, and without answering her inquiring looks as to who I was, I asked her to tell me her name.

"'Mary,' she said.

"'Ah! yes; Marie—Mary what?'

"'Just Mary.'

"'What is your papa's name?'

"'Charley.'

"'Charley what?'

"'Only just Charley. Mamma calls him only Charley.'

"'Well; what's mamma's name?'

"'Katy—Katy darling, papa calls her sometimes.'

"'Where is your papa?'

"'Don't know where papa is.'

"'How did you get in this boat?'

"'You see, when everything was shaking so, and the houses was falling, papa picked me up and run down to the river and put me into the boat; then he went back to bring mamma. Mamma was coming down the hill. When papa and mamma got down the hill the boat was way out in the river. As papa jumped into the water to catch the boat the big water come and run all over the bank and all over mamma. The boat rocked and shaked so bad I fell down in it, and didn't see papa and mamma any more.'

"Fully comprehending the dread catastrophe which had made an orphan of the dear little creature, I remained silent for several moments, when she asked me if she would see papa and mamma any more. I expressed to her my fears that she would not. Without undertaking to explain to her little mind the cause of the dreadful calamity which had happened to her papa and mamma, I told her that I would be a good papa to her, and that I would love and take care of her. The dear little creature evinced a clearness of mind unusual in one so young. She may have been as much as four years old. She had cried until the fountain of her tears had dried up. She soon became perfectly reconciled to her situation, and by degrees ceased to speak of papa and mamma. From all I could gather from her, I became satisfied that New Madrid was the scene of her misfortunes; the result of the great earthquake.

"I took little Mary to my hut. She soon learned to love me. As she grew up I sought to amuse and interest her little mind in every way possible. The wild-woods, with its beautiful flowers, and many changing scenes, afforded a wide field for the pleasures of her childhood. I taught her to read and write. She acquired all the knowledge I was capable of imparting. She was most fond of her little Bible, which she had read through and through more than a half dozen times. She learned to mark the Sabbath days, and to keep them more holy than other days. Her sanctuary was in the deep shades of the glen, and her pew the green sward, guarded by the halo of her own pure thoughts. Joyous and happy in her own Eden, she knew nothing of guile, and not a stran of one of her golden ringlets had been touched with evil. She lived in the pure atmosphere of her own soul, tempered by the teachings of the Virgin Mary; born to love, her loving nature went in search of something to love. On the lake she was most fond to dwell; communing with and caressing her little finny companions, she taught them a language of her own. Oh! she was so happy. The light and life of my old days, it was the resume of my younger and happy days.

"From the day that the handsome young hunter appeared to her upon the lake, from the hour when they parted under the shadows of the bluff by the spring, she seemed to live and breathe a different atmosphere; all that she had once loved and cherished became oblivious. She went no more to commune with and caress her little lake companions. She seemed awakened to a new and foreign life—love's imagination had possessed her very soul. 'Twas like our first mother, when the scales fell from her eyes and she beheld the first man Adam. The first evil had touched her and entered her pure soul, and made it flesh fleshy. The angel of the Lord came in the night time before she had changed her paradise on earth and rescued her pure, sinless soul and transported it to the paradise in heaven, by the side of the Virgin Mary. The White Lily was dead! dead! dead! the morning of the day she was to have joined her Adam on earth. As she lay upon her humble little couch the morning which to her was to be the brightest on sinful earth, when the first ray came over the bluff, reflecting its light upon her sweet face, her bright blue eyes had lost their glory—the angelic smile yet lingering upon her bright countenance pointed as an index-finger to a more glorious realm on high, to which her soul had taken its flight. 'Twere better so, or 'twere better far, that her little lake companions were alone left to moan her absence from the bright waters of the 'Lake of the Lilies.'

"Of myself I write, that I was born in France, on the fourth day of April, 1737. I was christened, in the holy Catholic faith, Pierre Saint Martin Nichol. My father was of honorable birth; becoming bankrupt by investing largely in John Law's Mississippi bubble, I was taken from school when in my seventeenth year. Of ardent and restless temperament, I joined an expedition fitting out for Canada, and will have lived in America on to-morrow—to-morrow! The light of my life has gone; my soul followeth to-morrow."

CHAPTER XI.

Haywood County—Colonel Richard Nixon, the Pioneer Settler—N. T. Perkins—Hiram Bradford—The Taylor Family—Major William R. Hess—His Appearance before the County Court—The Moody Excitement.

HAYWOOD—named for one of North Carolina's honored and trusted sons, Judge John Haywood—was erected into a county in the year 1821. One of the second tier of counties from the Mississippi river, lying between the waters of the Big Hatchie and Forked Deer rivers, it embraces within its limits a larger area of rich and arable territory than any other county in West Tennessee. The early immigrant settlers to it, were men of character and wealth, who shaped and modeled its institutions, and gave tone to society.

Among them were Col. Richard Nixon, L. McGuire, Nicholas T. Perkins; the Sanders, Taylors, Bradfords, Bonds, Estes, and many others, whose brave hearts and inflexible will sustain them in the perils and hardships of pioneer life, and who stand as among the noble fathers of the land.

The first court was organized and held at the house of Colonel Richard Nixon, on the eighth of March, 1824, by Richard Nixon, Laurence McGuire, Nicholas T. Perkins, Jonathan T. Jacobs, William Dodd, Britton H. Saunders, David Jeffries and

Blackman Coleman, Ricard Nixon being elected Chairman. The following officers were then elected: Britton H. Saunders, Clerk; John G. Caruthers, Sheriff; Richard W. Nixon, Trustee; William Dood, Ranger; Reuben Alphin, Constable.

The following named gentlemen composed the *venire* from which the first grand and petit juries were formed: Richard Nixon, Edward Howard, Charles Howard, William H. Henderson, Alfred Kenedy, John McWhite, Jonathan Nixon, Thomas G. Nixon, Lewis Welerby, Julius Saunders, John Johnson, John R. McGuire, John Jones, Nathan Bridgeman, S. W. Farmer, Hardy Blackwell, Wyatt Twity, Willie Patrick, R. W. Nixon, William H. Dyer, H. A. Powell, James York and Thomas Ghent.

The first order of the court was to the Sheriff, requiring that he collect the sum of six and three-fourth cents per every one hundred acres of land in the county, as a "fund to pay the tallismen and jurors one dollar a day."

The first Circuit Court was held on the fourteenth day of June, 1824, at the house of Colonel Richard Nixon; Joshua Haskell, Judge, and Blackman Coleman, Clerk. The first settler in Haywood, was

COL. RICHARD NIXON,

who blazed out his course and cut his own road from the settled vicinity of Jackson, to where he pitched his tent, on the creek which took his name (Nixon's creek), three miles east of Brownsville. The red men of the woods were encamped on the same creek—the noble Chickasaws—with whom he cultivated kindly relations, and for many weeks shared with them the hospitalities of their camp.

The first civil courts of the county were organized and held in his house, as also, the first religious meeting where prayer was made. As the county began to settle up, the hardy pioneer boys and girls would meet at his house and enjoy the old time dance. He was at the birth and naming of the county site, acting as one of the commissioners in laying off the town (Brownsville).

A member of the Magistrate Court from its inception, he was chosen as its chairman, which position he retained until his death in 1831. A novel case arising in the early courts of Haywood, involving a question of title to some land or free-hold, governed by the laws and adjudications of the courts of North Carolina, requiring a certain law book, which was not to be had or found in the law libraries of Tennessee, he mounted a courier on horse-back and sent him post-haste all the way to Raleigh, N. C., for the law book, and had it produced on trial of the case at its next term.

His last mingling among his fellow-citizens of Haywood, was as President of a Fourth of July celebration at Brownsville, a few months before his death, on which occasion the following volunteer toast was offered by a cotemporary settler, Mr. H. Haralson, and drank with hats off: "To Colonel Richard Nixon, President of the day. The FIRST SETTLER, AND MOST PROMINENT CITIZEN." Colonel Nixion was born in North Carolina in the year 1769. He represented the people of his native county,

New Hanover, with distinguished honor for many years. Noted for his genial hospitality, kind and generous heart as a neighbor, his name will ever be kindly remembered by all who knew him.

While it is not the purpose of the writer of these semi-historic reminiscences to become the biographer of all the old and worthy pioneer settlers in the Big Hatchie country, he cannot, without a breach of courtesy due the "old folks," whose long and eventful lives have come down to the more modern days, leave unnoticed the name of

ESQUIRE NICHOLAS T. PERKINS,

who, with a small colony of his name and kindred, immigrated from East to Middle Tennessee at an early day, and as soon as the way was opened up to the out-skirts of civilization, pressed on and settled in Haywood in the year 1823. In 1824 we find him one of the first acting magistrates, and one of the commissioners to lay off and establish the site for the seat of justice for the county, which he, in conjunction with the other commissioners, named Brownsville, in honor, it may be vanity to presume, of one of the North Carolina Browns.

In March, 1825, he acted as a commissioner with L. McGuire, Charles White, William H. Henderson and Thomas G. Nixon, under appointment from the Worshipful Court of Pleas and Quarter Sessions, as it was then called, selling at public sale the lots in Brownsville.

'Squire Perkins was born in Nox county, Tenn., A. D. 1793, and died in Brownsville in 1872, having lived six years beyond the period allotted to man, and within a few months of a half century in Haywood. Most exemplary in the moral, and without spot or blemish in the social, always faithful in trust for himself, he became the executor, administrator and guardian of more of the widows' and orphans' property and estates, than any man in the county, which attested the truth of the saying, that "he who managed his own affairs well, could be trusted to the fiduciary management of others." He enjoyed, to the last day of his long and useful life, the confidence of everyone, never betraying a trust. He discharged the various duties devolved upon him with marked business tact and capacity, and sterling integrity and fidelity. He died as he had lived—highly esteemed, respected and venerated.

Brownsville "was without form and void" until the opening of spring, in the year of our Lord one thousand eight hundred and twenty-five. "Goods, wares and merchandise" had been sold in Jackson from the establishing of the town, which was done in 1822—the town lots having been sold in August of that year. Brownsville was the next oldest county town, and had the honor of having the first store between the latter place and the Mississippi where a yard of tape or a paper of pins could be had, and

HIRAM BRADFORD

was the first store-keeper. He was long the leading merchant of the place and business man of the county. His long and eventful career is worthy, not only of a page in the early history and settlement of Brownsville, but of imitation by all beginners in hewing out the rough and difficult pathway of life, when self-reliance is the only sustaining element. In his youth, he had made it his aim and object in life to become rich, and to brave whatever of peril and hardship it might cost him in its accomplishment. He got his first start by trading in horses and mules, taking them to the old settled part of Louisiana, through the many miles of wild Indian territory, and often returning home to his father's house on the Cumberland, in Stewart county, on foot, when he would not see a white man's face from the settlement at Natchez until he reached Tennessee. In his frequent trips to Louisiana, he had examined the country, then in the cradle of the wilderness, from the Big Hatchie to the Yazoo, cultivated friendly intercourse with the Indians, and "talked injun" equal to a Chickasaw or Choctaw. Reaching the age when it becomes man's duty to "pare off" and assume the responsibilities of a good citizen, he married and resolved to fix his residence among the Tunica hills of Louisiana, where he had seen cotton growing. He went to work, in part with his own hands, and built him a flatboat, against the earnest protestations of his father and neighbors. Getting his boat ready by fall, he loaded it with corn, leaving room for his young family and household. So much opposed was his father and family, including his two negro men, to his moving to Louisiana, which was regarded as a sickly country, and to thwart his going, in the dead of night, before the morning fixed for his leaving, his flatboat was scuttled by the negroes and sunk in the waters of the Cumberland.

He rose early the next morning and repaired to the scene of his discomfiture. The people of Dover, a little town on the Cumberland where his father resided, gathered to the river bank. The boat was yet fast to the bank, and about one-half of the front part of it out of the water. Hiram pulled off his coat and with his two negro men went to work, throwing out the corn, which was in the after-part of the boat. Soon she began to rise, when he, with a face beaming with delighted hope, ran up on the bank, jumping high up and slapping his heels together, cried out: "Hurrah for Louisiana!" His friends, taking inspiration from his ardent and undaunted spirit, though loth to see him go, fell to with him, and by noon had the boat afloat and ready for loading up again. Filling it again with corn, and putting aboard his young wife and one child, with such comforts as would be needed on the trip, he, with his two negro men, cut loose the moorings and floated out from Dover in the fall of 1817. Meeting with no difficulty on the voyage, he floated down the Mississippi, landing at Bayou Sara, meeting with the first steamboat he had ever seen on the way.

With his two negro men, he labored in the cotton-field, succeeding well in raising cotton. The hot sun and long summers of Louisiana, together with the unhealthy state of the country, determined him to move back to Tennessee. Familiar with the rich virgin lands west of the Tennessee river, he resolved on fixing his future place of abode in Haywood. Learning the day fixed for the sale of the lots in Brownsville, he gathered together his accumulations, with which, and his cotton crop of ten bales of that season, he went to New Orleans and bought him a stock of goods, ordering his family to be ready on the bank of the river for the boat as she came up. Shipping his goods on the steamboat ——, and taking his family aboard as she passed up, he landed at Fulton in the latter part of February, 1825. His aim was to attend the sale of the lots at Brownsville. Procuring a couple of horses at Fulton, he mounted one of them, taking one child before him and another behind him. His wife rode the other, with the third child behind her. He started off for the lot sale, making his way as best he could along Indian trails, until he reached the neighborhood of Brownsville, stopping at Reuben Alfin's. He was among the first on the ground, when the sale of lots began, and bid off the first lot, No. 1, situated on the corner of the Public Square and East Main street, south side. Having his two men with him, he put them to work the next day upon a large oak tree that stood near the corner, which he had split into slabs, twelve by fourteen feet long, and built the first store-house erected in Brownsville. It was built over the stump of the tree that furnished the material for its construction. The Major, leaving his family with Reuben Alfin, returned to Fulton, and, by the time his new store-house was covered in and floored with puncheons, he had his boxes of goods ready on the ground to be opened.

During that year he erected a saw-pit on the same lot, and had sawed out by hand lumber with which he built the first hotel in the town, adjoining his store-house, which, for size and respectability, was not equaled by any house of public entertainment in the district. It was continued as the finest and best hotel in Brownsville until within a few years past, when it had to give way for the more modern improvement in brick and mortar. In front of his hotel, he set out the first shade tree on the Public Square, which also fell a victim to the progress of the age, to make room for a shelter of dry boards, the stump of which still clings to mother earth, to remind the passer-by of the hand that put it there, where for forty-six years it bloomed and blossomed (it was the flowering locust) over the front windows of the hotel, under which the gay young men of the town stood and coursed loving talk to the beautiful young women, daughters and sisters of the proprietors, long, long ago, through the raised windows and flowing curtains.

Few men lived so long and blameless a life as Hiram Bradford, enjoying the fruits of a well-earned fortune and an honorable name, all of which he left as a noble heritage to his surviving children.

THE TAYLOR FAMILY.

Five brothers of them, Richard, Howell, John Y., Edmond, and Buck, with the old patriarch, their father, migrated from Virginia in the year 1827–8, and made permanent settlements in Haywood.

Men of parts and large property, zealous in the advocacy and vindication of law and order, noted for their patriotic zeal and Christian virtues, none contributed more in the forming of sound morals and the general well being of society. Their lives were a noble example to posterity, illustrative of the passion that animates man in the character of a good citizen. The writer regrets his inability, for lack of sufficient data, to give such a personal sketch of the several members of the family as their long and useful lives so justly merit; as also, of many others of the old and first settlers whose names are worthy to be mentioned in these pages.

The first physicians who settled in Brownsville were William C. Bruce, Dorthel, Penn, Dillard, Johnson and Barby.

ALLEN J. BARBY'S

name as physician, citizen and benefactor stands alone in Haywood. One of nature's noblemen, he stands to-day without a living peer among his early professional associates. The writer, for lack of the necessary data, is unable to give such a personal sketch of Dr. Barby as his long and useful life justly merits. Few men, whether in the professional or private walks of life, have enjoyed the uniform confidence and esteem of his fellow-man more than Doctor Allen J. Barby.

DAVID MCLEOD,

the pioneer tailor of Brownsville, is yet among the living. Before the town had a corporate existence, he worked at his trade in a shop built of logs. To afford the necessary light to his tailor's bench, a side-log was sawed out. The old tailor, though bent a little with the weight of many years, takes pride in pointing out where the big stump stood upon which he used to build a fire to heat his "goose," with which he pressed off the first suit of clothes he made, for Colonel Nixon, from cloth bought out of Hiram Bradford's "rail-pen store."

DANIEL CHERRY,

with other owners of land grants west of the Tennessee river, had a drawing for choice of locations. Mr. Cherry drew the first and second choice, and as early, perhaps, as 1821, visited West Tennessee, locating his first choice where he afterward settled, on the Forked Deer river, and his second choice at "Poplar Corner." It was not, perhaps, until 1823 that Mr. Cherry fixed his permanent residence on the south fork of the Forked Deer river, where he early made his mark as a man of enterprise and thrift. His first aim in opening up the country, was to provide well the "staff of life." His choice of lands were unsurpassed in fertility, and particularly adapted to the culture of corn. He soon became noted as the best corn grower in the district. Corn and meat he always had to sell. The writer, in looking over the files of the Jackson *Gazette* (a newspaper published in Jackson by Colonel D. C. McLean), finds an advertisement of Mr. Cherry's, which, with his teeming fields of corn, shows the fatness of the land. The advertisement reads thus:

"BACON.

"I have about 15,000 pounds of bacon and 1000 pounds of lard for sale at Harrisburg, in Haywood county. DANIEL CHERRY.

"April 23d, 1825."

In another place in the same paper he advertises several thousand bushels of corn for sale. He showed great enterprise in the building of a mill on the Forked Deer, by which the surrounding settlements were supplied with good meal. Selecting his mill-site on a slough at the edge of the high land where he had fixed his residence, he built a broad levee across the bottom above the overflow, upon which the public could travel at all seasons of the year. To afford ample water for his mill, he contracted the width and consequent flow of the waters of the Forked Deer, causing an increased flow into his mill-pond.

By his probity and practical good sense he grew rich, and reared a large family of sons and daughters, many of whom, with their sons and daughters, live to adorn the society of West Tennessee.

Mr. Cherry was a native of North Carolina. He lived a long and useful life. His memory will be venerated as long as the place (Cherryville) which bears his name shall be known through future generations.

THE FIRST EXECUTION.

The first execution issued against personal property, and put in the hands of the Sheriff, Reuben Alfin, acting deputy was levied upon a male of the cow kind, a large red bull, belonging to the defendant in execution. The acting deputy felt kindly toward the defendant, and had made it his special business to make it known to all the people of the country the day on which the noble animal would be sold, and had spoken much of the property in execution, of his blood and pedigree, for he was of the best stock of cattle from Middle Tennessee. His owner had taken great pains in his raising, and handled him easy. The kind-hearted deputy had practiced with him some, in order that he might handle him to advantage on the day of sale. The day, according to the notices pasted up through the country, came around, and the bull was brought to town and tied to a large stump in the Public Square, with many feet of rope, to allow him the use of himself as well as to graze around. It was summer, and not uncommon in those days for the grass to grow on the square, or in the streets.

As the hour for the sale approached, the people from many parts of the country began to pour in, and gather around the bull, to examine and take a look before the sale commenced. He was a monster bull, a dark mahogany-red, without spot or blemish, fat and sleek—a prize to a modern butcher. The time arrived for the sale to begin; the good-hearted deputy mounted the stump, to which the property in execution was tied, and made proclamation of the terms of the sale, etc., and called for bids. Many cattle-raisers were there, and soon an active competition among the bidders sprung up. The good-hearted deputy sheriff kept up a lively crying of the bids, now and then pausing to expatiate on the fine qualities and immense value of the noble animal. In the meantime, the town folks gathered on the square and around the bull. Curiosity and interest on the part of the numerous bidders caused the crowd to press in close and around the bull, thus pushing him out to the extent allowed by the rope—some thirty or more feet from the stump to which he was tied. Comprehending nothing of the gathering and excited interest around him, the bull began to grow restive, shaking his great head and tearing up the ground. He was regarded as perfectly gentle and docile, however, and his becoming excited and animated only increased the interest of the surrounding by-standers. In the meantime the bidding increased in interest and rivalry, and was going on bravely, when a laboring man came out of a well that he was digging near, and, attracted by the crowd on the square, he pressed in to get a sight of the object of so much interest. The bull by this time had become infuriated. The well-digger continued to press through the crowd until he got within a few paces of him, as though he proposed "taking the bull by the horns!" No sooner did the infuriated animal get a sight of his red flannel shirt than he made a rush upon him. The man in the red flannel turned and made his best run to keep out of his way, taking his course circling around the stump, and for the most part on the outside of the bidders and by-standers. In the bull's run the rope slacked up, taking the crowd along about the knees. The bull had performed the circle, leveling every one to the ground who stood within it. The situation was becoming painfully terrific. The man with the red shirt kept on the outside, beyond the reach of the mad bull. The kind-hearted deputy, to relieve the situation immediately around him, pulled out his knife and cut the rope, freeing the bull, when he broke for the red shirt. Away they went amid the excited shouts of the crowd, across the square, the bull gaining on him every jump, until the well-digger reached his well, only saving himself by swinging on to the well-rope and letting himself down out of sight. The bull, finding himself at liberty to go his way, broke for home. The injury and damage around the stump was purely incidental, lacking in malice, and the bull was freely forgiven.

The last and highest bidder was not remembered by the deputy sheriff. The day for returning the execution was close at hand, and how to make his return upon it was a puzzle.

Had Vol. Sevier been a resident of the town at that day, it would have been said that he had had something to do with the well-digger's coming out of his well with a red flannel shirt on.

Prominent among the lawyers who early settled in Brownsville, was

MAJ. WM. R. HESS,

ingenuous and amiable in aspect, square in build and medium in stature; his hair, for lack of a barber, usually fell low upon his broad shoulders. In dress he was careless, sometimes to slovenliness. A good dinner and full bottle pleased him much. He had wit, learning and elocution, sprightly in debate, with all the dignity of a professional man, yet he was modest and retiring. Admitted to the bar when quite young, he soon took a high position, and gave promise of a brilliant future. Few men, in so brief a career, attained to a higher degree of eminence, or held within his grasp a power of mind that would have insured the full measure of a laudable ambition. His genius and learning, however, were counterbalanced by indolence and a too great fondness for personal ease and self-gratification. The public weal concerned him little, refusing on several occasions to accept positions, requiring him to mix with the *vox populi;* yet he was good company, and enjoyed the social of a small circle, and a good joke, not unfrequently perpetrating one himself.

It is remembered of him, that on one occasion he appeared before the Magistrate's Court—the Court of Pleas and Quarter Sessions—one winter day. He had just risen from a good dinner and an empty bottle, and remembering that he had a motion to make before the Court adjourned, he strode toward the Court-house. Losing nothing of his accustomed dignity of manner, with measured steps he walked into the court-room. Unbuttoning his old green blanket overcoat, throwing back the heavy colar, and thrusting his left thumb in the arm-hole of his vest, he presented himself to the Court, announcing his wish to make a motion. The Court, being engaged in some matter then before it, paid no attention to him. He announced again that he wanted to make a motion, yet the Court heard him not. Patiently he stood, the personification of the great Webster in the United States Senate. Raising his clear, ringing voice, he repeated, for the third time—

"May it please this most Worshipful Court, I

have a motion to make. Will you please hear?"

Still no recognition. Putting on his hat, he turned upon his heel and walked out of the court-room, with the same steady step that he came in. Passing out to a pile of brickbats that lay in the court-yard, he filled the great pockets of his over-coat, and retraced his steps to the court-room, with a brick in each hand, as well as one in his hat, and again presented himself before the Court.

"Now, Mr. Chairman," he said, "I will make a motion that will engage the attention of this Court."

Suiting his action to his words, he let fly at the Chairman's head. He dodged and fell under the Judge's bench, the brick shattering the window-glass behind him. The Major let fly another, and another, at the associate members of the Court, until his pockets were emptied. In the meantime, the "Mr. Chairman," who lisped badly, was all the while crying out to his associates:

"Lah loh, boyth, lah loh, all on you! He'll hit thom on you, if you don't lah loh."

The Major, after exhausting his ammunition, retired in good order, but the Court, apprehending his return with another pocket full of bats, ordered the Sheriff to adjourn Court, and they left the bench enjoying the last "motion."

"The Moody Case," occurring several years later, in which the Major figured, was the last case of any note in which he was connected. The case is memorable for the interest and excitement it produced in the county. It occurred in the days that Murrell and his clansmen figured, and Moody was regarded as one of the clan. As now remembered, it was a *prima facie case*, under the law, *of negro stealing*. A negro man, belonging to a highly respectable and worthy citizen of the county, Egbert Shephard, Esq., was missing from his master's premises. Whether decoyed off or "run away," was a question soon solved in the minds of the people, by the negro being caught in a watermelon patch somewhere between where his owner lived and the Mississippi river, and Moody, who had been "spotted," found upon the premises. The negro was brought back, and lodged in jail for safe-keeping, until the supposed negro stealer could be apprehended. Language is tame to say the county and town was in a blaze of excitement. The popular mind was in fever heat previous to the occurrence of this case. Negro stealing was becoming common, and the institution was becoming menaced and threatened in divers ways; so it was not long before Moody was brought for trial. The gathering on the Public Square that day was large, and the excitement and indignation surpassed anything that occurred before or since. The old and best men of the county were there ready to participate in anything that was necessary to be done, whether to hang the offender, or to keep him from being hung, without judge or jury. But, alas! for the offended law, proof of the right sort was lacking. Negro proof was not legal, and it was the only kind of testimony in proof of his guilt that could be offered. Yet in the minds and consciences of every one he *was* guilty. He plead not guilty, however—stood up with a bold and defiant mien, and challenged proof before the men of the law of the land and God! He vowed that he neither knew the negro by sight, nor did the negro know him.

It was arranged to put his avowed innocence to the test. The populace formed a ring, in the middle of which a number of men known to be strangers to the negro, together with Moody, was left standing. The negro was brought out of jail, and turned loose, and told to go in the crowd and find the white man who had decoyed him away from his master's premises. He passed in through the outer circle, and up to where Moody, with a dozen men, were standing, and, to the amazed astonishment of the would-be innocent accused, laid his black hand upon his shoulder and announced him to be the man. A scene ensued that beggars description.

Moody winced and wilted, while the populace with one voice announced him guilty. He was then taken in the court-room, and before the committing magistrates, the owner of the negro having made affidavit, and of necessity was the prosecutor. Maj. Hess had engaged to defend him. The court-room was jammed with the intensely excited and indignant citizens. In the meantime many of the old and young heads were in council on the other side. Negro testimony not being admissible under the law, and no other tangible proof at hand or likely to be found, the wise heads concluded that a trial before the courts would result in a failure, if not a farce, and resolved, upon his being discharged by the magistrates, to take the case in their own hands.

Upon the resolution being taken they proceeded to the court-room and awaited the action of the magistrates, who, upon their being no proof or witnesses produced, dismissed the suit against the offender. The court-room filled to overflowing—every man a witness in his own heart and conscience of the guilt of the prisoner. To see him discharged, to go hence without day, was grievously vexing. Just then a dozen or more of the leading bold spirits of the day rushed in with pistols in hand, leaping the outer railing, seized the culprit, and took him in their hands. The gallant Major, who had stood in his defense under the law, and who, by nature and instinct, was averse to the use of deadly weapons, gathered up his law books and announced to the *new regime* that he did not practice in their court.

The "case" was then opened upon a new hearing. The people threw themselves into a committee of the whole, upon their original sovereign rights, and drew from among themselves a panel of twenty-five jurors, before whom Moody was arraigned and put upon his trial. Sundry speeches and harrangues were made, inflammable and conservative. The drift of conscience sentiment was inflexibly that Moody was the veritable man, and a full verdict of "guilty" was rendered by the twenty-five citizen jurors. Failing to fix the penalty for so grave an offence, and being for the most part in favor of hanging, they recommended that another jury be drawn, composed of twelve of the most conservative and discreet citizens, who should fix the penalty, which was done, and constituted a part of the original proceedings.

According to the finding of the jury of his peers, the jury of twelve pronounced sentence according to the North Carolina laws; "that he be taken out and receive a given number of lashes upon his bare back, and be branded upon his left cheek with the letter 'R,' and required to put the Mississippi river or some other State line between himself and the State of Tennessee, within the twenty-four hours next ensuing." The sentence was fully executed, and Moody went according to the requirements of the people, acting in their sovereign capacity, and the "Moody Case" became history.

CHAPTER XII.

The First Steamboat—The Denizens of Haywood Gather on the Bank of the Big Hatchie to see it—Valentine Sevier, the Wit and Humorist of Brownsville—Cox, the Postmaster—Old Herring Bones—The Young Horse-Trader.

"Old times" in Haywood is memorable for many amusing incidents, anecdotes and "good things." Among the most amusing, and yet remembered with a lively interest, occurred on the appearance of the first steamboat that came up the Big Hatchie. Her coming was heralded over the county several days in advance, and the day she would be at the Brownsville landing named. All the men, women and children that could muster a horse or a go-cart (and many walked), turned out "to a man." A big *circus* or a *general muster* never drew a larger assemblage of people than was assembled on the banks of the Big Hatchie on that memorable day to see the first steamboat.

From Brownsville they had gone in procession order, with banners flying, led by the orator of the day, Major Hess, who had been chosen to welcome the Captain and his steamer, the Red Rover, in an appropriate speech. The day was propitious, and everybody that could go was there and in waiting. Every available twig, limb, sappling or stake, from the river bank for many yards back, was put in requisition to hitch and fasten the horses to.

For miles below the "puff" of the boat was heard. With steam up to the highest gauge, and every pound turned on, she came up "booming."

Along the river bank, on the bluff, and every available place for getting a sight, was crowded; many, for want of standing room, and to get a better view, got up into the trees. As the boat neared the landing, the press and anxiety to see—to get the first sight—became intense. Amid shouts and yells she hove in sight, turning the bend below with the last inch of steam turned in her cylinder, driving her keel through the swift waters of the Big Hatchie, to the amazing delight of the hundreds of anxious, throbbing hearts that stood upon the bank.

The dexterous pilot, judging well the place of landing as indicated by where the largest crowd was standing, with flying banners brought her to in a blaze of glory amid shouts of welcome. Running out her head and spring lines she was made fast. The populace pressed in close to get a better sight, as well as to hear the speech of welcome. Just then the engineer raised his valves and let off steam, and the scene that ensued beggars all description. Men, women and children broke as for dear life, some shrieking and screaming amid the deafening noise of the blowing-off sham, which had reached its culminating point in the boilers. The frightened horses had broken loose, where they could, and were tearing helter skelter through the woods and up the road, and those that could not break loose were rearing, pitching and dancing around the trees and places that held them. Everything looked as though the devil had broke out of his harness. Many were so badly frightened that they did not stop running or look back until they were out of breath, and the frightened horses never stopped until they got home.

The imagination of the reader may run riot in picturing himself such a scene as is here attempted to be described, which occurred in real life forty-five years ago. Not one in thirty of those who were there that day ever saw a steamboat, or knew anything about them save through scraps in the newspapers describing the horrible "blowing up" and destruction of life. It may be said that the "let-off steam" of the boats in those days was incomparably louder than now, and was as frightening then as a "blow up" would be now.

The reception proceedings were broken up for that day. The Captain and his officers were tendered a dinner at Brownsville the next day, where the Captain was welcomed and toasted. A cotemporary of "old times" promised to furnish a copy of Major Hess' eloquent speech on that occasion, which is yet preserved. It is to be regretted that it could not be obtained, together with the proceedings of that memorable day, and find a place in these pages.

Life, when viewed through the dim vista of bygone days with attending incidents, often appears as a curious piece of fiction wrought from a feverish, dreamy brain. The boys who walked four or six miles (survivors of that vast gathering) to see the first steamboat, whose quick and elastic step is now touched by gout or stiffened by the long walk of time, yet retain a lively recollection of the amusing incidents and scenes of that day, while little hillocks and white stones mark what remains of the middle-aged and old, save the fond memories of affection and love.

Valentine Sevier, a wit, humorist and practical joker of no mean order, yet lives in the memories of "old times in Brownsville." A decendant of the old stock of Seviers, who began life in Tennessee when it was "the State of Franklin, he inherited his full share of the genius of his forefathers, with the wit of his mother. Brave and generous, life with Vol was ever in the merry sunshine.

The town was never out of a joke—a fresh one for every day when times were dull—during his residence in it; the old and young came in for a measure of his wit. His manner, so frank and candid, yet grave and intensely pious when need be, that the victim of his jokes of yesterday, would fall into his trap set for him the next day. An old and respected citizen was F. S. Cox, long the postmaster at Brownsville. Cox had his personality, bordering on excentricities. Kind-hearted and generously submissive to whatever of fun that grew out of a joke practiced upon him, he not unfrequently conceived himself the *real* personage of a witty pun, or become seriously affected in imagination, by an innocent and harmless incident. So unsuspecting was his generous nature, that he often became a victim to Vol's jokes. Among the many amusing jokes perpretrated upon him, the following, in some degree, illustrates the man. One August afternoon he was returning from his dinner, when near the public square, he came to a little white fice dog and another little dog grining and growling at each other on the sidewalk. In passing, they were in his way; he gave the little white fellow a rough shove with his foot, when the little dog turned and grabbed him by the calf of his leg, pinching him a little. Passing on, he paid no further attention to it. Vol Sevier was standing in Charley Guyger's store door and saw it. Picking up a double-barrel shot gun that set near, he sliped out the back door, and made his way around through an alley, and came up in a hurried walk to where Cox was just joining a crowd in front of the postoffice, inquiring aloud, as he came up, if any one had seen a little white fice dog. Passing up to Cox, he said:

"Mr. Cox, did you see anything of a little white fice dog on your way down from dinner?"

"Yes," says Cox, "if he belongs to you, Vol, you'll find him down there," pointing to where he had seen him.

"No," says Vol, "he is not mine, but I am after him to kill him; he is mad!"

"Mad! did you say?" says the postmaster, gathering up his leg—"mad did you say?—hydrophobia! hydrophobia!" he cried out, jumping upon one leg, holding on to the other until he reached the nearest seat. "Tench, Tench, my son, I am bitten by a mad-dog, my son. Oh! hydrophobia! hydrophobia! run my son for the doctor, and tell him I am bitten by a mad-dog."

Tench obeyed, and the postmaster hobbled in the back room, holding on to his bitten leg. In the meantime Vol slipped around and intercepted the doctor, and gave him the cue. The friends of Cox had gathered around him, not suspecting the joke, and wanted to see where and how he had been bitten.

"No," said Cox, holding on to the calf of his leg with both of his hands, "wait until the doctor comes."

The doctor soon came in with a smile in his eye. Cox related to him the manner and how he was bitten, laying himself flat of his back on a cot for the doctor to examine his leg. His pantaloons were carefully drawn off, his drawers turned up above his knee, and the doctor went to work to examine the fatal bite.

"Whereabouts is it," says the doctor.

"Right there," says Cox, putting his hand on the calf of his leg.

"Well," says the doctor, "take your hand away, and let me examine it."

The doctor looked and examined, but could find no bite or sign of a dog's tooth.

"Why, Cox, there must be some mistake. There is no mark of a dog's tooth on this leg."

"Yes he did bite me, and that must be the leg; it was the nearest to him—there is no mistake about it, I am bitten by a mad-dog. I am sure that I am bitten, for I felt it when Vol Sevier told me the dog was mad."

"Who told you the dog was mad?" says the doctor, with a grip upon his risable.

"Vol Sevier; he was after him with a double-barrel."

The doctor could hold in no longer, bursting into a laugh, he said:

"Why, Cox, you are only bitten by one of Vol's jokes, there is no sign of a dog bite on your leg."

The good-natured postmaster realizing the hoaks, dressed himself and joined his friends in the joke.

Vol played a joke off on old Robin, a notable character of "old times" in Brownsville. Robin was familiarly known as "Old Herring Bones," an appellation he inherited from his native State, North Carolina. His early raising was near the herring shoals of the old North State. He indignantly resented the *slam* upon his nativity. Known and respected for his age and fidelity to his owners, he became a sort of free man about town and a privileged character. The old negro swore like a trooper; and when provoked his tongue knew no bounds. Robin always walked with a long staff—sometimes it would be a corn-stalk. When the boys about town would find Robin with his corn-stalk, they would poke fun at him by calling him "Old Herring Bones;" when he would lose his self-command, and chase them to the school-room, or some safe place of retreat. Robin claimed revolutionary honors—that he served, with his old master, Macon, in the Revolutionary War. He was brought to Haywood by George Jordan, stepson of Colonel Nixon, and last belonged to Colonel Mansfield Ware, who, venerating his age and past faithful services, allowed him great latitude about town.

On one occasion he bought for Robin the cloth for a fine suit of clothes, and told him to take it over to Eddings' tailor shop and get Mr. Eddings to take his measure and cut them out, and his mistress would have them made. Robin took the cloth and walked across the square to Eddings' shop. Mr. Eddings was out. Vol Sevier happened to be in the shop at the time.

Robin, after waiting some time, began to get impatient for Eddings to return. Vol inquired of him what he wanted with Eddings. Robin told him that the Colonel had bought him cloth for a suit of clothes, and sent him to Mr. Eddings to have his measure taken and the suit cut out.

"Well," says Vol, "Robin, if you are in a hurry I can take your measure, and when Mr. Eddings comes in he can cut them out."

"What! you tailor, Vol Sevier? You no tailor; no, sir; can't spile this cloth, that you won't."

"But," says Vol, "Robin, I can take your measure and the tailor will do the cutting."

Vol's manner of speech became convincing, and removed old Robin's doubts as to his ability to take his measure. He finally consented, if he would be in a hurry and do it quick, as the Colonel would be waiting for him.

"Well," says Vol, "take off your coat and vest." Robin did as he was told.

"Now take off your pants and shirt, Robin," says Vol.

Robin faltered, and began to doubt whether Vol knew what he was about. Vol soon convinced him, however, that he did, and he consented to take off everything he had, if Vol would only be in a hurry and let him off quick.

The old negro denuded himself of his shirt and breeches.

"Now," says Vol, "Robin, get up on this broad table; it was made for the purpose." Robin did as he was told.

"Now lay flat on your back."

Robin obeyed as a medium in the hands of a mesmerizer.

Vol straightened and fixed Robin's legs and arms, and taking a piece of chalk commenced taking his measure. Beginning at Robin's head, he traced around and down his neck to his shoulder, then down his arm and round up to his arm-pit, then down his body and around his hip down to his heel, thence up the inside of the leg and down the other leg to the heel, thence up the other side as before to the beginning.

Just as he was making the finishing mark, Colonel Ware stepped to the door and asked for Robin. The old negro raised himself up in a sitting posture. The Colonel, comprehending in a moment what Vol had been at, commenced scolding Robin for allowing himself to be made a fool of by Vol Sevier. Robin, realizing his situation all in a moment, commenced cursing Vol, jumped off the bench, and gathered his long staff. Vol, understanding old Robin when he thought fun was being poked at him, leaped out of the front door and "Old Herring Bones" after him, and the Colonel calling to old Robin to come back and put on his clothes, an old fool, and go home.

It was several months before Vol Sevier would let old Robin get within reach of him.

"Old times" in Brownsville had its tailors, saddlers, tanners, ginmakers, and shoemakers, but was without a barber. The tailors, on account of their handling the scissors well, were often called on to do the hair-cutting; sometimes the dexterous young clerks, who always had sharp scissors, were called on. Vol in his kind offices toward his fellow-man, learned to handle the *scissors*, and was regarded as the best hair-cutter in town, and was often called upon when he was not in the *humor* for the job. It was only his partial friends, and they were many, that he would barberize.

There came to Haywood, most every fall, a handsome young man from Middle Tennessee, trading in horses and mules. He had made the acquaintance of the young men about town, and, withal, was an agreeable young man, and a pleasant companion. He dressed well, rode a fine horse, and always had money in his pocket. He was admitted into society—just enough to admit of his making the acquaintance of a few young ladies.

His hair needed cutting very much; learning that Vol was an expert hair-cutter, he hunted him up. Vol, with a half dozen or more gentlemen of leisure, were sitting under the shade trees, before Welch's tavern, when the young man came up. Approaching him, he said :

"Mr. Sevier, I learn from your friends in town that you are in the habit of cutting hair, and that you are the best cutter in town; will you cut mine?" Vol threw his humorous laughing eye upon the handsome young trader for a moment before replying.

"I hope I am not mistaken in the gentleman; your friend Mr. Cox, the postmaster, pointed you out to me, and told me you were the best hair-cutter in town, and that you would cut it for me."

Vol had decided, telling the young man to go over to Eddings' tailor shop, and get a pair of scissors. The evening was pleasant, and by the time the young horse-trader returned with the scissors, the crowd under the shade trees had increased in numbers. The young man returned, his face beaming with delight. Camp-meeting was going on out at the camp-ground, and he wanted to look his best the next day. Vol rose and fixed his chair for the young man to sit in, who, taking off his coat, fixed himself straight up and was ready for the operation.

Vol pulled off his coat, and commenced without asking him how he wanted it cut. His hair was long and bushey, and inclined to be redish. Vol combed it out straight, parting it in the middle from his forehead to the nape of his neck, and commenced on one side where it was parted, and worked down to his ear. As the scissors clipped off the last long lock on that side, the crowd around looking on, began to giggle and snigger. The young man, devining that it was something about his head they were amusing themselves at, put his hand up to the *barberized* side, and feeling no hair, he bursted out into a rage of flaming words, jumped up and swore that it was an outrage—"that he had rather than the price of his fine horse, not to have had his head ruined." Vol, in his bland manner, without a smile, while the bystanders were in a roar of laughter, persuaded the young man that his hair was not "ruined," and before he cut the other side, to walk in the public room of the tavern, where he would find a looking glass, and he would see that it *was not "ruined."*

The young trader took him at his word; went in and saw himself in the glass, as others had seen him. He grew furious and uncontrolable; swore and cursed at Sevier, and everybody else, but particularly at Cox, for recommending him as a hair-cutter.

He swore "if anybody would fight him, he would fight the whole town."

All the while Vol kept his face unwrinkled, persuading the young man, who had become wild with passion, to take his seat and let him finish the job.

But no! he would not. He vowed that "he should not put his hand on his head again or cut another hair."

The joke had taken rather deep root, and seemed likely to become serious. However, Vol possessed great fertility of expedient, and he was bound to work out of it. Few men knew better the workings of the human passions. A master performer exercised not more power over his instrument than he did in mastering the springs of feeling and thought of his subject, or with whom it was his wont to play. His joke had taken well, and he was willing that it should go forth as a *preventive* to future annoyances in the way of hair-cutting. Letting the young trader rage and fume until the mirthful crowd were satisfied (which satisfied him), remaining all the while without a wrinkle or reflex from his face to show that it was purposed, he threw his enchanting coils around his green subject, and seated him again, for the other side of his head to be done likewise; and when finished, convinced the owner of a well shaved head that it became him admirably, which was attested by those around turning their mirth into admiration of his dexterity in handling the scissors.

Sevier took much interest in things about town, and frequently contributed to the interest and variety of the local trade. To exemplify his passion in that way, an anecdote is preserved of him, in which he caused his friend Cox to become the contributor. Cox was concerned in the tanning business, and was the largest purchaser of green hides in town. It was customary to weigh and sell the *horns* with the hide at the established price. Vol happened to be down at the tanyard one day when a lot of hides belonging to an honest, hard-working countryman were being weighed and delivered. He noticed one of them without horns—the hide of a *muley* cow or ox. The country gentleman took the weight of the hides and went up town to get his pay from Cox. Vol went along with him. Going along, he suggested to the owner of the hides that he was entitled to *hornage* on one of his hides.

"What?" says the countryman, "how! what did you say?"

"*Hornage*," says Vol. "One of your hides was a muley—didn't have any horns. It is worth more than those with horns. So, when Mr. Cox goes to pay you, you must claim hornage."

The hide vendor understood it. Handing in the weights, the calculation at so much a pound was made and the money being counted out, when the country gentleman stated to Mr. Cox that he was entitled to hornage on one of the hides—that it was a muley hide.

"Hornage! what?" says Cox; "who ever heard of such a thing as hornage?"

"I have," says the gentleman seller, "and you have got to pay me hornage on that muley hide."

In the meantime Vol stepped in, and his friend Cox appealed to him, to know if such a thing was ever heard of before, and what he thought about it.

"Yes," says Vol, "it's right." "Hornage" was established in the tanyard thereafter, upon Vol's decision.

CHAPTER XIII.

Fayette, Its Geographical and Topographical Features—County Sites Established for Seven Counties—L. P. Williamson—Hardeman—Bolivar—Ezekial Polk—Jackson—Colonel C. D. McLean.

FAYETTE.—The year after the Chickasaw title to the lands in West Tennessee was extinguished by the United States government (in 1818), by an act of the Legislature, the territory embracing the present limits of Fayette, Hardeman, McNary and Shelby, was attached to Hardin, and comprehended Hardin county. Afterward, and during the period of the same session, by a supplemental act, the present limits of Shelby was defined and fixed.

In 1821 Shelby county was established, and the territory now forming the counties of Fayette and Tipton, was attached, and Hardeman and Haywood attached to Madison.

In 1822 Hardeman was established, then embracing the territory, which, the year following (1823), was laid off and erected into a county, and called "*Fayette*" in honor of, and for

GENERAL LAFAYETTE,

who, the year following, was the "*nation's guest.*"

In the year 1824, the counties of Fayette, Hardeman, Haywood, Tipton, Dyer and Gibson, became separate and independent counties, with separate judicial jurisdiction. Previous to that period, and up to 1821, the inhabitants of the territory, now Fayette county, were embraced within the jurisdiction of Hardin; and from 1821 to the period when it was established as a separate county, under the jurisdiction of the courts of Shelby.

In the same year (1824) commissioners were appointed by the Legislature to locate and establish county sites for the new counties embraced in the act of that year.

In 1825, Somerville was established as the permanent county site for Fayette, and the lots were sold by the commissioners, appointed by the county court, in September of that year. It is worthy of note, that the county sites for the counties of Haywood, Tipton, Obion, Hardeman, Gibson, Dyer and Fayette, were located and established in the same year. Commissioners by the several county courts were appointed to lay off the towns and sell the lots, the several sites having been located upon grounds donated for that purpose.

The commissions for Brownsville, Haywood county, were L. McGuire, N. T. Perkins, William H. Henderson and Thomas G. Nixon, and the sale took place the *third Monday* in March.

The commissioners for Covington, Tipton county, were Marcus Calmes, Robert G. Green, John Eckford, Alex. Robinson and E. T. Pope; sale twelfth of April.

The commissioners for Dresden, Obion county, were John Terrell, John Schultz, Mear Warner, Perry Vincent and Martin Lawler; sale fourteenth of April.

For Bolivar, Hardeman county, Thomas J. Hardeman, John H. Bills, Nat Steel, West Harris and John T. Cockran; sale on twenty-second of April.

For Gibsonport, Gibson county, J. B. Hogg, William C. Love, John W. Evans, Robert Finkle and John P. Thomas; sale July twentieth.

For Dyersburg, Dyer county, J. Rutherford, Griffin Rutherford, Ben Porter, William Martin and Thomas Nash; sale twenty-sixth of July.

Commissions for Somerville, were Henry Kirk, Daniel Johnson, Hamilton Thornton, William Owen and John T. Patterson; sale on the fourteenth day of September.

During that year (1825) immigration to the new counties exceeded any other year.

Fayette—the territory embraced within the limits of Fayette, bordering north on the waters of the Big Hatchie, south by the pure silvery waters of the Wolf, the Loosa Hatchie, with its numerous feeders, rising up through the center—no county in West

Tennessee was more inviting to the early immigrant settler, or could boast of richer virgin lands, peculiarly adapted to Southern agriculture, and capable of sustaining a large population. Settled by men of enterprise, intelligence and wealth, it early took a stand among the most favored counties in the district, noted for the refined, cultivated taste and good morals of its citizens. Prominent among the early *pioneer settlers* of Fayette worthy of honorable mention, and whose long and useful life, beginning with his early manhood, was the late

LEWIS P. WILLIAMSON.

With an energy and enterprise unknown to the present age, he exchanged the luxuries and comforts, the pleasures and enjoyments of a cultivated and refined society in the "Old North State" for the hardships, dangers and difficulties incident to the early settlers in the wilds of West Tennessee. His boyhood days spent in his native State, North Carolina, his early manhood at "Yale," where he graduated with honors in his twentieth year; he returned to his native home, an elected member to the State Legislature before he was twenty-one years of age. Nine miles northwest of Somerville he fixed his residence, in the loveliest spot in the wilderness, and built him a *round-log house with a passage in the middle*, like other new comers of that day, and called it "Ivenness," after a place in Old

Scotland, from which his wife's ancestors emigrated, where he with his happy family lived, improving and beautifying it until his death, which occurred in 1865, having lived three score and four years, and the last forty in Fayette.

Mr. Williamson was a ripe scholar, a polished writer, an eloquent speaker and ready debater. He several times represented his fellow-citizens of Fayette in the State Legislature with notable ability. He was the author of, and secured to West Tennessee the first railroad charter, the Memphis and LaGrange railroad; which was afterward adopted, and formed a part of the Memphis and Charleston railroad.

In the early days of Whigery he entered the field of politics, under the banner of "Harry of the West," and became a candidate for Congress. His glowing eloquence in the cause of Whigery—in advocating and maintaining the principles of government as taught by the great statesmen, Webster and Clay—distinguished him as a man of merit, and eminent among the first men of West Tennessee. Noted for his refined, cultivated taste, strict moral deportment, and his utter abhorrence of "grog-shops" (he was a great advocate in the cause of temperance), he relied alone upon his personal merit and the justness of his cause for votes. In the celebrated canvass in which he made a distinguishing mark as a speaker and ready debater, C. H. Williams, of Madison, and W. C. Dunlap, of Shelby, were his opponents. Williams was of the same school of politics with himself, and Dunlap a Democrat. Mr. Williamson and Mr. Dunlap made the canvass of the district together, on horseback. Personally warm and fast friends, an anecdote is told of them, illustrative of the men and mode of electioneering. Traveling together one day, they came to a cross-roads store, where liquor was kept also. Colonel Dunlap, forgetting nothing of the qualities constituting a successful canvasser for votes, discovering several men standing in the store door, halted as they rode up in front, remarking to his friend Williamson that he felt dry—that if he, being a temperance man, would hold his horse for a moment, he would get down and "take a drink." The kind Mr. Williamson readily consented.

Colonel Dunlap dismounted, and with a generous, smiling face entered the store. Calling for a drink, he turned to the bystanders, and said:

"Gentlemen, join me—candidate for Congress—passing through your country—glad to make acquaintances. Come, gents, join me in a drink."

He was of course joined by half a dozen or more hardy voters, they thinking it was their *rightful* duty to drink a candidate's liquor. While all were filling their glasses and exchanging glances at each other, the Colonel, throwing his eyes across his shoulder, remarked:

"See that man on his horse? He is a temperance man; delivers a fine temperance speech. He wouldn't be caught in such a place as this for all the votes in the neighborhood. He is my opponent. My name is William C. Dunlap, candidate for Congress—good day, gentlemen; I can't be with you longer; my friend is holding my horse."

Mr. Williamson's devotion to the case of Whigery induced him to retire from the canvass in favor of his political *confrere*, Colonel Williams, when his prospects of election were considered brighter than any other candidate in the field. His compass of mind fitted him for every intellectual pursuit. His rare business capacity and refined cultivated taste was evidenced in the management of his agricultural and domestic affairs and the beautifying of the home of his family.

It was, perhaps, in the year 1856–57, that the Agricultural Bureau of the State offered a prize for the best agricultural essay and address on the occasion of the Fair held that year at Jackson. The contestants were Governor James C. Jones, Governor A. A. Brown and Lewis P. Williamson. The prize was awarded to Mr. Williamson, and ordered printed in the report of the Agricultural Bureau.

As a Christian gentleman, worthy and honorable

in every pursuit in life, no more fitting tribute and eulogy upon his fair name and character could be offered than the following quotation the writer is permitted to make from a touching letter from his widow, after his death, to a friend, and who survived him but a few years. She says:

"From the period of his conversion throughout his whole life he was a Christian in the sublime and exalted spiritual sense of the word, and was ever ready to give a reason for the faith that was in him with meekness and fear. While his worth was like a *heap of gold that could not be counted*, the great characteristic feature of his noble nature was his disinterested benevolence. From the time he left college up to the close of his useful life, he had the care of the widow and the orphan, managed a great many estates for rich and poor, and never accepted compensation save in one instance, when it was forced upon him. His labors of love and works of goodness were abundant, and known only to the few, for all were done in a quiet, unostentatious manner, not letting his left hand know what his right hand did. But his work is with his God, and his record is on high!"

HARDEMAN.

In 1822 Hardeman was formed, and the counties bordering on the Hatchie extending to the Mississippi, including Shelby, were attached for judicial purposes. The courts were held at "Hatchie Town" until 1824, when Bolivar was laid off and established as the county site. The county was named for Thomas Hardeman, member from the *county of Davidson* to the first territorial convention, held at Knoxville on the 11th of January, 1796, to frame a constitution preparatory to Tennessee becoming a State, and the town of Bolivar was called for the great "liberator of his country," Simon Bolivar, the hero of South America.

BOLIVAR

was a Venezuelean, born in Carraccas in the year 1785. Of noble blood, he was educated in the refined courts of Europe, a companion and traveler with Humboldt. When in his twenty-sixth year he returned to his natal land, offered his services to the Congress of Grenada to rid his country of the Spanish yoke, and with six hundred men marched against the great Spanish General Morillo. After eleven years struggle with varied successes, he finally triumphed over Morillo and his Spanish troops, confirming the title which had been given him of being the "liberator of his country."

Noted among the first settlers in Hardeman was

COLONEL EZEKIEL POLK.

The advanced age to which Colonel Polk had attained when braving the trials and hardships incident to pioneer life; in bringing the ax and plow where alone the savage hunter's footprints had trod the wilderness—the haunts of the wild beast—marked the strong and inflexible will and indomitable energy of the man. Colonel Polk's early life, his habits and proclivities, had fitted him for such an undertaking. A revolutionary patriot, he had served with the rank of Captain and promoted to that of Colonel in our struggle for independence.

He was a member of the first convention held in South Carolina to take measures against British encroachments. With a widely-extended and intelligent understanding, he displayed a sound judgment in the management of his affairs, marked with strong idiosyncrasys of character, as was notably attested by his writing his own epitaph. As a curious piece of literature of "old times in the Big Hatchie country," it is here reproduced for the amusement and interest of the reader, without comment:

"Lines to be inscribed on the grave-stone of E. Polk, written by himself June 24th, 1821, in the seventy-fourth year of his age:

"Here lies the dust of old E. P.,
One instance of morality;
Pennsylvania born, Carolina bred;
In Tennessee died upon his bed.
His youthful days he spent in pleasure,
His latter days, in gathering treasure;
From superstition lived quite free,
And practiced strict morality.

To holy cheats, was never willing,
To give one solitary shilling.
He can foresee, and foreseeing,
He equals most men in being.
That church and State, will join their power,
And misery on this country shower;
The Methodist, with their camp-brawling,
Will be the cause of this downfalling;
An error not destined to see,
He waits for poor posterity;
First fruits and tenths are odious things,
And so are bishops, tithes, and kings.

As there are no rocks in this country fit for grave-stones, let it be done on durable wood, well painted, and placed upright at my head, and a weeping willow planted at my feet."

The Colonel died three years afterward; this, among his last injunctions, was obeyed.

JACKSON.

Jackson, Madison county, the abode of ease, elegance and refind civilized enjoyment, the homes of the interprising and intelligent, the beautiful and cultivated, the seat of learning and temple of the law, was the *first habitable* town in West Tennessee. It was peopled before Brownsville, Covington, Somerville, Bolivar and other county towns, had a local habitation, or a name, by the best families, from the old States. It was there the first courts of law were organized and the first academy of learning established, and gave birth to the first *newspaper* published in West Tennessee. It stands to-day, with its blocks of brick and mortar, fashioned in the most approved taste and style of modern architecture—its fine public buildings, and private residences, with its enterprise in manufactures and commerce, thrift and wealth, second only to Memphis, with its many more advantages, beside the great "inland sea," rolling past its front. Yet it is within the recollection of the writer, when it was but a hamlet on the banks of the south fork of Forked Deer, dependent for its *sugar and coffee* upon the navigation by "keel boats" of that little tortuous stream. It is regretted—the more to be regretted, as "old times in West Tennessee" had its birth at Jackson—that the reminiscences and incidents of early life in that place is debarred its full share in the pages of this little volume. Should the *theme* which has engaged the pen and interest of the writer, find favor with the readers of these "reminiscences in the Big Hatchie country," he may be encouraged to a larger and more inviting field, which will take Jackson and Madison county as the starting point, and "work up the timber," according to the original "blazes." The apology, if indeed, an apology be necessary, for going to Jackson, is to make honorable mention of one of the pioneer newspaper men of West Tennessee (and the first paper published in the district)

CHARLES D. M'LEAN,

"the best in the world," whose long and usefu life has been spared through the vicissitudes and gradations of establishing a country, wrought from the wilds of a savage territory into a highly improved State, teeming with wealth and population—the work of only a half century. But few men are older, and who have been longer connected with the early and late history of West Tennessee than Colonel McLean. A native of Virginia, he was born in the year 1795. Emigrating to West Tennessee, he settled in Jackson in 1823–4. On the twenty-ninth day of May, 1824, he, with Elijah Bigelow, issued the first number of the *Jackson Gazette*, which was continued to be published under his supervision and management until the year 1830, when it came under the editorial management of the late J. H. McMahon, and its title changed to that of the *Truth Teller*. The *Gazette* was the immediate successor to the *Pioneer*, the first newspaper published at Jackson, which ceased to be published after the death of its editor, occurring in a few months after the first number was issued.

The *Gazette* was the only paper published in the district for several years. It was published in the interest of General Jackson and David Crockett, from 1824 to 1830 inclusive; the files of which is yet preserved by Colonel McLean as a relic of "old times" in West Tennessee, and is a welcome guest among the "Old Folks at Home," of which he is their honorable President, and ranks the oldest. Colonel McLean was honored by a seat in the State Legislature, from the county of Madison, during his residence in that county. In the year 1833, he fixed his place of residence in the vicinity of Memphis, where he continues to reside. Having lived to a green old age, his venerable form, beginning to bend a little with the weight of many long years of usefulness, may be seen on the streets of Memphis every bright day, enjoying life in a good joke, "the best in the world," which is the Colonel's universal response to an old friend, when inquiring as to his health—it is always the "best in the world."

CHAPTER XIV.

Bright and Lastiug Memories of Youth—Linking the Past with the Present—The Old Log Schoolhouse—The School-Path and Play-Ground—Demanding a Day's Holiday—Barring Out the Schoolmaster.

The most lasting of memories graven upon the young mind—the scenes and incidents of young life—become brighter and fresher in after life, linking, by fond and endearing memories, the past with the present, forgetful of the long intervening years of pain, peril and strife. With the vision of the past, the aged look back through the dim vista to the days of their youth, as a bright thrilling dream, enchanted by its memories, as a lover in pursuit of the object of his affections—bright pictures upon the unstained walls of youthful memory most truthful in nature.

The old schoolhouse, where they first learned to "spell baker," the play-ground with its scenes and incidents, the big spring and the sparkling spring-branch, rippling over its pebbly bed through the deep shades of the forest to the creek, where at summer's-noon they learned to "swim;" the school-path, narrow and winding through pleasant grounds made hard and smooth by the daily tramp of many little feet; the "foot-log" across the deep creek, where they were wont to stop and cast pebbles into its bright waters, or amuse themselves with the schools of little fishes rising to the surface to gather the crumbs from their "school-basket;" the five and thirty "school boys" banding together, to demand of the "schoolmaster" a day's holiday to go to a log-rolling or house-raising; or, perchance, to a fish-fry, or a shooting match, and he, in his individual sovereignty protesting against their juvenile wishes—their natural rights. The final decision taken, the early gathering of the boys at the "schoolhouse;" the barring of the doors and windows; the anxious waiting, and appearance of the "old schoolmaster," as he rises the hill; his wroth and angry will at being barred out of his rightful castle, and being dethroned of his authority—he demands entrance, denouncing the "assumed rights," declares it a revolt, and threatens vengeance upon the leading rebels; the whole school backs up the leaders, while they stand pleading through the open cracks in the logs, disclaiming ill-will, and expressing their perfect willingness "to submit to his rule and discipline to-morrow;" the schoolmaster still refuses, holds on to his iron will, and renews his threats of punishment; he *riles* the boys to more desperate measures; the final catastrophe culminates, the doors are unbarred, and the five and thirty heretofore obedient scholars gather round the schoolmaster, a half dozen of the largest gather him up upon their shoulders, and he is borne away to the creek—the usual place of going in swimming. The old incorrigible kicks and writhes, threatening vengeance; the pool is reached, and the whole school cry out, "souse him—souse him; it will cool him off;" the hard-hearted "schoolmaster" begins to soften; the tyrant begins to beg and promise to let them have the day. Too late, too late, souse—he goes under! "Souse him again!" by the whole school. Imploringly he cries, "stop! hold! do it no more and you shall have a week's holiday." That will do—let him off, let him off," was the verdict of the school. Smiling and good natured he clambers up the bank, and all hands join in expressing good will, with promises to be punctual to school Monday morning, and study hard.

The most joyous and happy gatherings of the neighborhood, in "old times," were at the quiltings. It was seldom that the young people in the settlements got together except at a quilting frolic. During the early winter months a week never passed without a quilting, which always ended in a dancing frolic, followed soon by several weddings. It was common, during the "log-rolling" season, for quilting to be going on at the house while the men were out in the field or new-ground rolling logs. It was usual to invite the whole settlement to a log-rolling —the men to come and bring their wives and daughters. It was always the occasion of a big dinner. The field-work done, and the quilt finished, everything was cleared away for the hardy young men and girls to have their frolic. A fiddler who could play two or more tunes was always on hand. It would puzzle the "pleasing recollections" of "old times" to treasure up the varied innocent country amusements that brooded over the land. The fair and happy country lass thought not of making herself beautiful by art. Her plump, glowing cheeks put to blush the face-physic, common to "dressy" young women of the present day. Unwittingly they romped and played, unmindful of the outside tissue or tinsel; decked in innocence, she doth all things sweet and graceful;

"———— to paint the lily;
To throw a perfume on the violet,
———— to add another hue
Unto the rainbow ————
As wasteful, and ridiculous excess."

OUR MOTHER.

Gentle reader, the strongest and most enduring passion of the human heart is for OUR MOTHER.

"All other passions fleet to air."

Sweet, endearing memories of our mother, who

loved us ere we had a being, from whom we drew our young life—thy image, the brightest engraven upon "memories wall," becoming brighter—unfading and undimmed by time, is embalmed in the heart's affection. That little hillock raised upon the bosom of mother earth, overgrown with green moss, or decked with flowers, marks her last resting place; it has for us a resistless charm—we would not ask

> "——to give us back our dead;
> Even in the loveliest looks they were."

Through all the wanderings and varied mazes our wayward feet have trodden since our youth, the image and sweet memories of our mother endeareth; growing brighter and more lovely as the hair upon our heads takes upon it the frosts of many, many winters.

Reader, are you ever reminded of your mother, unbent and stately—stately among the stateliest, with elastic step, easy under the weight of venerable years—as she moves with an ear at all times kindly open, and a heart generous, loving to the prattle and whims of her children's children, her grand and great grandchildren, in their shining new frocks and clean white aprons, vieing with each other as to who should do this or who that for her? They were very *sunshine* to her in the vale and shadows of her last days. Such are the sweet memories of *my* mother when last I saw her in life. May I not claim, in filial respect to her memory, the mention of her name in these pages as one of the brave-hearted mothers and wives who shared with their husbands and sons the perils and hardships of the pioneer settler's life in the Big Hatchie country? It would be filial impiety not to.

Born and reared in the lap and ease of plenty, she, when fortune's frowns were most bitter, joined with her husband—my father—in the wish to seek *new faces* and a *new home* in the far off West. Leaving behind all painful regrets, with the true heroism of a wife, she followed the fortunes of her husband through the long and wearisome travel from Cumberland county, North Carolina, through the sands of South Carolina, Georgia and Alabama, to Covington county, Mississippi, taking camp fare and camp comfort common to the *movers* of that day (1822). With no misgivings as to the future, always cheerful and joyous, sustained by a pure Christian soul undimmed by adversity, she felt rich alone in the objects of her affection—her husband and children—her six little jewels, the youngest an infant and the oldest but twelve years. Sojourning a few years in Mississippi, she enters the same vehicle in which she had traveled from the "Old North State," with her *six little jewels* and *another* added, and shared the *mover's* comfort through the Choctaw and Chickasaw "nations" to the Big Hatchie country, as mentioned in the first chapter of these reminiscences.

My mother, whom my father was fond to call *Patsey*, was born in North Carolina, December 26th, in the year 1790, and was christened Martha Macon. Macon was the maiden name of her mother. She was the fifth child of Joseph Seawell and Martha Macon, and third daughter, and next to the youngest, who was a son. Their names were Harry, James and Nat, *Nancy* (Ann), *Betsey* (Elizabeth), and *Patsey* (Martha), my mother. She survived them all—her brother James only a few years.

My mother married my father in the year 1806, when in her seventeenth year. Under her loving care five sons and three daughters grew up to man and womanhood. She lived to enjoy the society and mingle in the domestic circle of her children until all had grown old together, and to *bless with her fondest love and affection fifty-six grandchildren*, *beside great grandchildren.*

She survived my father by thirty years (remaining a widow), her youngest child (a daughter), nine years, and eldest (a son) by two years, and was by *her surviving children* followed to her last resting place in Elmwood, April, 1867, having lived seventy-seven years and seventeen days. Zealously attached to her church (the Presbyterian), of which she had been a member sixty-one years. Loving, kind and charitable, exercising charity toward the uncharitable, she was notable for her deep piety. With strong intuitive love for her children, she closed her eyes to their many shortcomings, while her soul was in prayer in secret. If to be blind to the faults and frailties of one's children be sinful, it was my mother's greatest sin. Loving, jealous, she watched over them with the same care and affectionate attention, as when they were around her footstool as little children.

It is difficult for the writer, in this short personal sketch of his mother, to separate her moral from her intellectual character. In her personal, she was a fair representative of the true majesty of WOMAN, spirited and gay in society, eloquent and chaste in conversation, tempered with feelings of tenderness and respect for the opinions and fancies of others. She was always the welcome guest in the social of her friends and acquaintances.

The genuine sentiment of her loving, kind, and generous nature, combining all the charming accomplishments that so beautifully adorn the Christian daughter and sister, wife and mother, distinguished her as a NEIGHBOR.

Ardent in her temperament, devoid of fickleness, she was firm and constant in her friendships; devoted to her Bible, her religious feelings grew stronger and her faith brighter in the evening of her long life.

The truths and beauties of the Christian gospel were fully illustrated in her death, as they had been exemplified in her long life. Such, gentle reader, was one of the pioneer wives and mothers, who enjoyed life in the first settler's cabin and among her neighbors, who "spun cotton and wove cloth," long before envy and jealousy, common to fashionable life, entered the settlements—who lived to see the wilderness disappear for the broad cultivated acres, the finely constructed mansion take the place of the settler's cabin, and refined cultivated taste brood over the land, where the howl of the wolf, and sharp, startling scream of the panther first became familiar sounds. Such was my mother, who, in life, was highly esteemed, and enjoyed the society of many friends, and whose memory is embalmed in the hearts of her surviving children.

An incident occurred in connection with my mother's last and mortal illness, vouched for by members of the family, which, however, it may encourage the dogmas of *spiritualism*, is deserving of mention. My mother's late residence in the town of Somerville was a retired and quiet *cottage home*, beautifully improved, and fashioned after her own taste and fancy, and for the most part by her own hands. "*My little cottage home*," she was fond to call it.

Upon the mantle in her room stood an old time clock; it had been a *companion in time* with her for near a half century. For several months previous to her death, the old clock had refused to run. Several repairers of clocks had tinkered at it, yet it would not go—it refused to make time any more—it worried my mother. She finally gave up the undertaking of making it *run*, and left it with its weights sitting loose inside the case. A few days previous to her death she rode out to her daughter's, several miles in the country; it was on a Monday she went out. Tuesday night at about eight o'clock the members of the family who were sojourning with her in her "little cottage home," were startled and amazed by the "striking" of the old clock. Sitting in an adjoining room (there being no one in my mother's room), they, in mute astonishment, followed the strikes until it *struck twelve*. Some minutes afterward, and while the members of the family were speaking of the unaccountable incident (for every adult member of the family were aware of the abandoned condition of the old clock,) a messenger rapped at the door, announcing the sudden illness of my mother, and for a doctor to be sent in haste. At *twelve* o'clock the day following the morning, she *breathed her last*. Connected with this incident, and which made it the more impressive and sad, she had sent in on Tuesday morning, writing a note, for certain articles of dress and material to be sent, which she desired should be made up and ready for *shrouding her mortal remains.*

Our mother! 'tis but thy mortal life death can sever;
Thy sweet image lives embalmed in our heart's affection forever.

www.ingramcontent.com/pod-product-compliance
Lightning Source LLC
LaVergne TN
LVHW010210110826
845151LV00004B/1044
9781425528683